D0875519

BEST-KEPT SECRETS OF
TUSCANY

Publisher and Creative Director: Nick Wells
Project Editor: Sara Robson
Picture Research: Sara Robson
Art Director: Mike Spender
Digital Design and Production: Chris Herbert
Layout Design: Mike Spender
Proofreader: Amanda Leigh

Special thanks to: Chelsea Edwards, Victoria Lyle, Cat Emslie and Claire Walker

12

5 7 9 10 8 6

This edition first published 2008 by
FLAME TREE PUBLISHING
Crabtree Hall, Crabtree Lane
Fulham, London SW6 6TY

www.flametreepublishing.com

Flame Tree is an imprint of Flame Tree Publishing Ltd.

© 2008 this edition Flame Tree Publishing Ltd.

ISBN 978-1-84786-231-0

A CIP record for this book is available from the British Library upon request.

All rights reserved. No part of this publication may be reproduced, stored in a retrieval system, or transmitted in any form or by any means, electronic,
mechanical, photocopying, recording or otherwise, without the prior permission in writing of the publisher.

All photographs courtesy of and © Hugh Palmer, except the following: © Hugh Palmer, from *The Most Beautiful Villages of Tuscany* by
James Bentley (Thames & Hudson; London and New York, 1995): 3, 4–5, 9, 50, 52, 53, 56, 59, 82, 87, 88, 114, 127, 140, 155, 157, 167, 168, 176, 182, 184;
and courtesy of Shutterstock and the following the photographers: *6015714281* 96, 99, 103, 192; Natalie Adamov 5 (t), 100; Alexey Arkhipov 13; Danilo
Ascione 21, 67; Darren Baker 118; Rob Bouwman 44, 68, 69, 111; Bertrand Collet 20, 119; Claudio Giovanni Colombo 33, 104, 134, 141; Andrea Danti
162; Nicholas Peter Gavin Davies 18; edobric 6, 66, 129; Herbert Eisengruber 37; Maurizio Farnetti 150, 189; Jake Foster 117; Martin Garnham 70; Andrzej
Gibasiewicz 163; Happy Life 23, 26; hipproductions 137; Coia Hubert 16; Javarman 142–43; Jbor 60, 62, 63, 64, 120, 131; Kevin H. Knuth 65; Chua Kok
Beng Marcus 128; Massimo Merlini 7, 126, 135, 145, 148; Paul Merrett 19, 29, 125; Sergio Nasi 164; Andrei Nekrassov 25; Mikhail Nekrasov 17; NEO 38;
Knud Nielsen 77, 147; Morozova Oksana 108, 110; Gijs van Ouwerkerk 14; Bruno Pagnanelli 22; Ph. W. 130; Philophoto 30; Viktor Pryymachuk 166;
pxlar8 15; Eline Spek 144; Manuela Szymaniak 132; Ricardo Tavares 73

Every effort has been made to contact copyright holders. In the event of an oversight the publishers would be glad
to rectify any omissions in future editions of this book.

Printed in China

Tamsin Pickeral (author) has studied art and history of art since she was a child, and lived for some time in Italy furthering her appreciation
of the subject. She now specializes in books on art and horsemanship with recent publications including *The Horse; 30,000 Years of the Horse in Art; The
Horse Owner's Bible; 1001 Paintings; The World's Greatest Art: Turner, Whistler, Monet; The World's Greatest Art: Charles Rennie Mackintosh* and
The Encyclopaedia of Horses and Ponies. She was also the author of Flame Tree's *The Secrets of Britain* in this series.

Hugh Palmer (photographer) is one of the world's leading photographers of landscape, architecture and gardens. His work has been
published in many magazines and reviews, including *Harpers and Queen, Country Life* and *The World of Interiors*. He has also carried out
a host of book commissions including many titles in the *Most Beautiful Villages* series published by Thames & Hudson, covering
locations all over France, Britain and Europe.

BEST-KEPT SECRETS OF
TUSCANY

Tamsin Pickeral

**FLAME TREE
PUBLISHING**

CONTENTS

CENTRAL TUSCANY 112

SOUTHERN TUSCANY 158

INTRODUCTION

At the heart of Italy is Tuscany, a magical and breathtaking land, unequalled in beauty and still echoing with the distant whispers of a history that stretches back to antiquity. It is a place of contrasts, of vertiginous mountains to the north, plunging river valleys in the north, east and west, and wide rolling plains and small conical hills in the central and southern areas. Dense forests – chestnut, beech and the ever-present cypress trees – unfold into criss-crossed vineyards, working their way across the countryside, and ancient, gnarled olive groves. Great tumbling rivers, the Arno, the Tiber and the Serchio, surge across her lands, while smooth, glassy lakes shimmer invitingly, and thermal springs bubble. Tuscany is richly fertile, producing Italy's most famous wine, Chianti, and the venerated olive oil so closely associated with Lucca, a Roman city within Renaissance walls. The land yields crops and sustains huge flocks of sheep and, to the south particularly, cattle. Tuscany is in its truest essence 'the land of milk and honey'.

This sense of richness and abundance is paramount too in Tuscany's cultural, historic and artistic past. There are few places where the past remains so indelible; in Tuscany the hills seem to breath with her history. The Etruscans were the first 'great' civilization to tame Tuscany, and the evidence of their life here from the eighth century BC is still visible, particularly to the south of the region that stretches from the western slopes of Monte Amiata, westwards to the picturesque coastline and south to the border with Lazio. It is here that they founded some of their most important cities, such as the coastal Populonia where

there is a sombre Etruscan necropolis, melancholy tombs of giant stacked slabs of stone and many artefacts, or little Saturnia with her thermal springs whose waters' curative powers have been lauded for centuries. Following in their footsteps, the Romans developed many of the Etruscan towns, and the Roman influence within Tuscany is strongly felt. Many of her towns still follow their original Roman layout with their main piazzas occupying the former Roman forum. A striking example of this is in Siena, the jewel of central Tuscany, with her Piazza del Campo, or Lucca in the north of Tuscany whose

streets follow a Roman grid plan. Another is the small coastal town of Ansedonia in the south, first called Cosa and established by the Romans in 300 BC. The Roman walls, complete with 18 defensive towers, still survive and encircle Ansedonia, which is entered through the Porta Romana, still beautifully preserved.

Strategic placement of towns for defensive purposes was a primary consideration, and consequently the majority of towns and even tiny villages were built within fortified walls and placed on the top or sides of hills. Routes for travel and communication were paramount in this respect, and crossing Tuscany from south to north are two of the finest Roman roads, which weave their way through the olive groves and vineyards. The Via Cassia travels from Rome northwards and into Tuscany, past the beautiful and hidden town of San Quirico d'Orcia and Siena, and on to Florence and Fiesole, while the Aurelian Way snakes from Rome north along the picturesque Tuscan coastline to Pisa and Lucca. Later, in the Christian era, the Via Francigena was built, almost parallel to the Via Cassia, to give passage to pilgrims travelling from Northern Europe to Rome.

One of the defining aspects for city, town and village design was defensive capabilities, and perhaps nowhere more so than in the heart of Tuscany where seemingly perpetual battles for power were fought between those who controlled the main cities of the area, Florence and Siena, striving to take control of, or protect, the surrounding satellite settlements. Furthermore, there were protracted struggles between the *Ghibellines*, who supported the Emperor, and the *Guelphs*, who were papal supporters, during the twelfth and thirteenth centuries. The defensive nature of Tuscany's settlements is striking; small villages, hidden away and far from the beaten track, cling to hillsides, which

offered far-reaching views of approaching enemies, and were less susceptible to malaria. A distinctive feature of these settlements is the Rocca, the fortress or castle, that is most often seen at the top, looming over the village, watchful and defiant, serving as a reminder today of the power struggles of years past. Castiglione di Garfagnana in the north of Tuscany has a particularly striking Rocca, built in 1371 by the Lords of Lucca, while Castelnuovo di Garfagnana in the lush Serchio Valley is presided over by its twelfth-century Rocca. In eastern Tuscany, the beautifully preserved medieval town of Lucignano is guarded by its fourteenth-century Rocca. This small town was the scene of constant strife as alternately Siena, Arezzo, Florence and Perugia fought for its control. There are few excursions to be made in Tuscany that do not take in more than one Rocca, standing defiantly against the skyline and wearing its history as a crumbling cloak of moss-covered stone.

plains that spread south of Siena in central Tuscany, have a unique appearance. Small conical hills, often topped by villages, rise up out of the landscape and horizons are punctured by rows of dark cypress trees. These areas were often painted by the artists of the Renaissance and can be distinguished in the backgrounds of many famous paintings. Montalcino is a village that appears to sprout from the top of a small hill and is surrounded by the vineyards famous for their production of the Brunello di Montalcino wine. Pitigliano is another hilltop town, though this time far in the south of Tuscany. This town sits on the top of a volcanic outcrop, buildings and town apparently seamlessly melded to the rock on which they sit. The defensive qualities of such a site were recognized by the Etruscans and Romans, who first settled the spot.

The area around Florence that spreads then to the west of the region and down to the coast lapped by the Ligurian Sea is dominated by the Apennine Mountains and boasts the Arno river, vineyards and olive groves. Here amidst the rich and vibrant landscape sits Florence, centre of the Renaissance arts, and Pisa, with her gravity-defying campanile. To the east and stretching towards the border with Umbria is a corner of Tuscany largely taken up by the province of Arezzo. It is a beautiful area presided over by the Apennines and the Casentino forest; tiny ancient and medieval villages are dotted amongst the trees, built on the mountainsides, with the stunning Camaldoli Monastery, begun in the eleventh century, being of particular note. The area is named after the city Arezzo that once rivalled Florence in power and wealth. Arezzo is the art jewel of the east, birthplace of both the humanist Petrach (1304–74) and Giorgio Vasari (1511–74), and home to a stunning collection of Piero della Francesca's (c. 1412–92) frescos.

The north of Tuscany is the most dramatic of her landscapes. The Apuan Alps and Garfagnana Mountains dominate, with great river valleys and huge densely forested swatches. Here the villages cling to the sides of rocky inclines, often their steep streets turning into steps upwards, and buildings seemingly jostled one on top of the other. The village of Cutigliano, nestled within chestnut trees and precipitously built, high in the mountains overlooking the Lima Valley, is just such a place, as is Montefegatesi, little more than a hamlet hidden amongst the sheer slopes. In contrast is central and southern Tuscany, where the landscape is more pastoral, with rolling plains, small hills and lakes. The Crete Senesi, with its grey clay soils that run south and east of Siena, and the beautiful Val d'Orcia, with her chalk

Despite her ancient history and magnificent display of architectural styles, it is as the birthplace of Renaissance art and architecture that Tuscany is most famous, with Florence being central to this. By the thirteenth century Florence was a hugely wealthy city, with much of her money based on banking. The Medici family owned the largest bank, and with this came power. During the 1430s they became the area's most powerful family, a position held for over 300 years, and in 1559 they led the Florentine forces to victory over the republic of Siena, and instigated Cosimo I de' Medici (1519–74) as Grand Duke. The Medici stamp is seen across Tuscany in the magnificent buildings that they commissioned and their coat of arms, which was often added to the exterior of existing buildings or monuments. Throughout this time Florence had become a centre of the arts, the humanities, literature and culture, and is home today to one of the largest collections of Renaissance art works and

architecture, not least in Filippo Brunelleschi's (1377–1446) Duomo of 1463. The influence of Florence's artistic awakening spread to the surrounding villages and towns of Tuscany, such as Volterra with her lovely campanile thought to be by Andrea Sansovino (1460–1529) or Lucca with her Renaissance city walls, or Pienza, a model town of Renaissance planning and architecture, and eventually through the rest of Italy and into northern Europe. Tuscany is full of Renaissance treasures, some expected, such as those within the great cities of Florence, Siena and Arezzo, and others utterly surprising. The palazzos tucked away in the country, hiding within acres of olive groves or woods, the churches, architecturally stunning, in tiny hilltop towns and the paintings secreted in long shadows within buildings far from the beaten trail; to some these unexpected and happened upon masterpieces are the true jewels of a land drenched in a cultural and artistic heritage as beautiful as her natural landscape.

FLORENCE & WESTERN TUSCANY

The majestic river Arno, silver-blue and at turns tranquil and enraged, snakes westwards from the rugged Mount Falterona in the Apennine Mountains down and across a great swath of country to the Ligurian sea.

Roughly following the Arno's time-worn path and amongst the river valleys and plains is an area of western Tuscany that is home to some of the most beautiful cities and villages in the world. This relatively small corner of Italy conceals a treasure of artistic, architectural and geological wealth, the vibrant countryside of stretching olive groves, vineyards and rolling hills matching in natural terms the mass of manmade jewels.

The sense of history here is great. It is a rich and vibrant history that is visible at every turn; relics from past ancient civilisations, the Etruscans and the Romans, poking up through the verdant landscape from the Etruscan walls of old Volterra to her Roman amphitheatre, the fortified towers of Vicopisano still defiant and Florence's Ponte Vecchio, her oldest bridge saved from destruction on Hitler's orders. Florence dominates with her incredible collection of art, the heart of the Renaissance still beats strongly here, but every small town and hamlet in this area also tells a story, with art and history concealed within the cool, mellowed buildings of years gone by.

TOWARDS THE CITY
AND RIVER ARNO
Florence

The beautiful and ancient city of Florence with her soft-
coloured buildings and skyline of spiky church spires spreads
along the banks of the river Arno. Her colourful history
stretches back to 59 BC when she was first settled as a
Roman colony, quickly becoming an important hub of trade
and commerce. It is as an artistic centre, however, that
Florence is most famous. During the Middle Ages she was
home to some of the greatest Renaissance artists and
intellectuals, and today remains one of the art capitals of
the world.

DUOMO AND SURROUNDING BUILDINGS

Possibly even more beautiful when seen floodlit at night, these are some of Florence's most distinctive and iconic buildings. Together they rise above the city, omnipotent and symbolic of Florence's commercial, political and artistic power. The cathedral's cupola, which was built by Filippo Brunelleschi (1377–1446) and finished in 1463, is one of the world's largest brick-built domes; incredibly it was constructed without the use of scaffolding. The campanile is some 6 m (20 ft) shorter than the dome, though equally impressive, while the octagonal baptistry is thought to date back to the fourth century in part, and is home to Lorenzo Ghiberti's (1378–1455) magnificent bronze doors.

DUOMO FACADE

The great cathedral of Santa Maria del Fiore (known as the Duomo) is one of the largest of its kind in the world. The initial plans were designed in 1296 by Arnolfo di Cambio (c. 1240–1300/10), although the architect died before the building was complete. The project was taken over by Giotto di Bondone (c. 1267–1337) in 1334 who designed the campanile with its distinctive bands of marble in pink, green and white. Following Giotto's death a series of architects worked on the building and by 1418 it was almost complete with the exception of the cupola. The facade of the cathedral as it appears today was not designed until 1871, and was completed in 1887 to reflect the patterned marble exterior of the campanile and the baptistry.

MICHELANGELO'S DAVID
Florence

In 1501 Michelangelo (1475–1564) was commissioned by the Arte della Lana (the Guild of Wool Merchants) to create a statue of David. The work became one of the most famous and brilliant renditions of a much reproduced subject, and is still today one of the world's most recognized sculptures. Michelangelo broke from the traditional representation of David seen after his victory, and chose instead to depict the young man in the moments before his fight with Goliath. He stands visibly tense and perceptibly concentrating on his impending confrontation; a figure that is both beautifully crafted physically, and also full of psychological depth. He is the ultimate symbol of bravery and power, both being qualities reflective of the city of Florence.

PALAZZO VECCHIO
Florence

The Palazzo Vecchio (The Old Palace) was originally called the Palazzo della Signoria and was designed in 1299 by Arnolfo di Cambio (c. 1240–1300/10), with later additions made in the fifteenth and particularly the sixteenth century. The building with its massive fortified aspect, projecting gallery and asymmetrical tower is very distinctive, and is still used as a town hall, in line with its original function as the seat of government. It was also used as the temporary residence of the ruling Ducal family, until the 1540s when Duke Cosimo I (1519–74) moved to the newly built Palazzo Pitti. It was at this point that the name of the palace was changed to Vecchio.

NEPTUNE FOUNTAIN
Florence

This striking fountain sits in the Piazza della Signoria in front of the imposing Palazzo Vecchio and was commissioned to celebrate the marriage of Francesco de' Medici (1541–87) and Johanna of Austria (1547–78). The piece was designed primarily by Bartolomeo Ammanati (1511–92) with help from his assistants, most notably Giambologna (1529–1608) who created the bronze Water Nymphs and Tritons. The central and impressive figure of Neptune in white marble represents Florence's power at sea, his face also bearing resemblance to Cosimo I de' Medici (1519–74). On completion the fountain was met with some hostility by Florentines, but went on to become an important model for future fountain designs.

UFFIZI
Florence

So often buildings photographed at night become even more magical, and the Uffizi is no exception. Home to some of the world's most beautiful and impressive art works, the building itself is also quite breathtaking in appearance. It was commissioned by Cosimo I de' Medici in 1560 to house his magistrates' offices, with the architect Giorgio Vasari (1511–74) in charge of the design. The plan of the building is horseshoe-shaped in layout, with one long wing to the east, a short bottom portion that borders the river Arno and a wing to the west.

BASILICA DI SANTA CROCE
Florence

The impressive neogothic facade of Basilica di Santa Croce was designed in 1857 by Niccolò Matas (1798–1892), although the church has a long history dating back to 1294, when it was built to replace an existing building. The Franciscan church is the largest of its kind and is particularly famous for being the final resting place of some of the greatest artists and intellectuals, including Michelangelo, Galileo Galilei (1564–1642), Niccolò di Bernardo dei Machiavelli (1469–1527) and the composer Gioachino Antonio Rossini (1792–1868). Amongst the art treasures inside Santa Croce is a beautiful series of frescos by Giotto and his pupil Taddeo Gaddi (c. 1300–66).

PONTE VECCHIO
Florence

Ponte Vecchio is Florence's most distinctive bridge, and also its oldest; it was the only bridge in Florence to survive the Second World War, and was allegedly saved on Hitler's specific instructions. It was designed in 1345 by Taddeo Gaddi and spans the river Arno at its narrowest point, where it is believed that a bridge had existed since Roman times. Shops still line the bridge, and above these on the eastern side is a corridor, the Corridoio Vasariano, designed by Vasari in 1565 to allow the Medici family to traverse the river without coming into contact with the public.

BOBOLI GARDENS
Florence

The Boboli Gardens stretch behind the Palazzo Pitti and across the gentle slopes of the Boboli Hill, and are today one of Italy's most famous and elegant parks. They were commissioned by Cosimo I de' Medici after he bought the Palazzo Pitti in 1549 and were created in honour of his wife, Eleanora di Toledo (1522–62). The initial plans were laid out by Niccolò Tribolo (1500–50) whose symmetrical and harmonious garden design became an important model for subsequent formal parks and gardens. Tribolo died before the Boboli Gardens were completed, and his work was taken up by Ammanati, Vasari and Bernardo Buontalenti (*c.* 1536–1608). The gardens are particularly noted for their sculptures and Roman antiquities.

LEANING TOWER
Pisa

This extraordinary tower must be Italy's most famous, and is the campanile to Pisa's duomo and baptistry. The structure was begun in 1173 with building work progressing slowly. By 1274 only the third storey had been completed, but already it was starting to tilt. Despite this, work continued on the tower and by 1350 it was finished, still leaning. The problem lay in the sandy and unstable subsoil of the foundations, and the tower has continued to keel during the years, leading to several restoration projects, the most successful of which was completed in 2007.

VIEW FROM THE TOWER
Pisa

The ancient and beautiful city of Pisa is perhaps most famous
on account of its leaning tower, but during the Middle Ages
it was one of Italy's main centres of commerce and was home
to a powerful navy that held dominance over the western
Mediterranean. By the twelfth century it had become an
incredibly wealthy city based on its strong trade links with
Spain and North Africa, and this wealth is reflected in the
magnificence of the city's buildings. In 1284 however, Pisa
suffered defeat to Genoa and later fell to the Florentines, but
it was during the Second World War that it suffered the most
when it was severely bombed by the Allies.

CAMPO DEI MIRACOLI
Pisa

Translated literally as 'Field of Miracles', this beautiful square green area is home to Pisa's duomo, baptistry and campanile (leaning tower), with the Camposanto stretching behind the baptistry. The imposing duomo dominates the space with its grey stone and white marble four-tiered facade, which is typical of the Pisan-Romanesque style. It dates to 1064 and was designed by Buschetto (*fl.* 1064–1110), whose tomb can be found in the left arch of the facade. The bronze doors of the duomo were cast in 1180 and designed by Bonanno Pisano (*fl.* 1170s–1180s), who is thought to have been the first architect to work on the campanile.

CAMPOSANTO
Pisa

The Camposanto (Holy Field) stretches behind the baptistry
and is one of the most beautiful cemeteries in Italy. The area
is enclosed by majestic pale marble cloisters, which form a
narrow rectangular building. Beneath the soaring closed
arcades of the cloisters are tombs, while other tombs can
be found in the central grassed area. The soil of this verdant
and tranquil space is reputed to have been brought by ship by
the Crusaders from Golgotha, the Holy Land. The walls of
the cloisters were once covered in a series of frescos made
over a period of several hundred years, including *Stories of
the Old Testament* by Benozzo Gozzoli (*c.* 1421–97), though
many of them were destroyed by bombing during the
Second World War.

RIVER ARNO
Pisa

The majestic Arno river weaves its way from the Tuscan Mount Falterona in the Apennine Mountains south to the Ligurian Sea, passing through two of Tuscany's most beautiful cities, Florence and Pisa. Pisa, situated on the coast, spreads along the banks of the Arno just before it reaches the sea, her elegant and mellowed buildings lining the river's edge. Pisa was once a great maritime power, and the only port along the coastline between the then small towns of Genoa and Ostia. Her decline, which began in 1284 with her defeat by Genoa, was then compounded by the silting of her harbour.

TORRE DELLE QUATTRO PORTE
Vicopisano

Approximately 15 km (9 miles) from Pisa is the ancient town of Vicopisano, nestled between the fertile hills of a valley that was once home to the river Arno. During the Middle Ages Vicopisano was a thriving and wealthy community, and the town's surviving medieval towers attest to this affluence. The Torre delle Quattro Porte (Tower with the Four Doors) is one of the more unusual of the towers and was once a fortified gateway into the old castle, and a watchtower. Dating to the end of the twelfth century, the tower was built in four stages, using different materials, which can still be distinguished today.

PARISH CHURCH OF SANTA MARIA
Vicopisano

The beautiful and ancient church of Santa Maria, also known as the Parish Church of Vicopisano sits in the vast Campo di Santa Maria, a large grassy area outside the castle that was used as the local market place. The church is the most important and the oldest of the religious buildings in Vicopisano; in its present form it dates to the twelfth century, although an earlier church is thought to have existed on the same spot. Unusually the church sits beyond the walled enclosure of the town, with its main entrance facing the castle gates, instead of facing west as is typical of religious buildings.

PAMPALONI FOUNTAIN
AND COLLEGIATA
Empoli

The agricultural town of Empoli lies between Florence in the heart of Tuscany and Pisa along her coastline. The area was settled in early Roman times, and grew quickly through its trade along the river Arno. The beautiful Pampaloni fountain, designed by the artist Luigi Pampaloni (1791–1847) sits in the centre of the Piazza Farinata degli Uberti and in front of the town's main church, the Collegiata di Sant'Andrea. The square is named after the Italian nobleman, Farinata degli Uberti (d. 1264) who is considered by some to be a heretic, based on his opposition to the pope. He was leader of the *Ghibellines* who supported the Holy Roman Empire, and eventually defeated the papal forces, taking over control of Florence.

TOWARDS THE VILLAGE
Artimino

CHURCH OF SAN LEONARDO
Artimino

The small, fortified hamlet of Artimino is surrounded by the most exquisite Tuscan countryside, with rows of gnarled olive trees and fertile vineyards stretching as far as the eye can see. Perched on the top of a small hill, Artimino affords panoramic views; it is a location that was first settled by the Etruscans and later, in medieval times, built into a walled and fortified hamlet, as it now appears. Sitting just above the town is the beautiful Medici Villa, while just beyond lies the Tumulus of Montefortini where excavations have revealed a two-chambered Etruscan tomb.

This ancient church sits guarded by tall and dark cypress trees, whose shadow provides welcome relief from the hot Mediterranean sun. The unspoilt and carefully restored Romanesque church, which was dedicated to San Leonardo, was founded by Countess Matilda of Tuscany (1046–1115) in 1107, though an earlier religious building existed on the site. Beneath the brilliant unblemished blue of the Tuscan sky the church resides as a fine example of a Romanesque structure, and is surprisingly imposing in relation to the size of Artimino. The magnificence of the building would have been a reflection of the wealth and power of the church's formidable founder.

VILLA OF A HUNDRED CHIMNEYS
near Artimino

Not far beyond the boundaries of Artimino and slightly
above the hamlet sits the Villa di Artimino, also called the
Villa of a Hundred Chimneys. The impressive house was
commissioned by Grand Duke Ferdinando I de' Medici
(1549–1609) as his hunting lodge, and was built by Bernardo
Buontalenti (1536–1608) in 1594. The number of chimneys
that punctuate the roofline is impressive, and lends the
building a quirky and endearing quality, rather at odds
with the magnificence of its structure. Buontalenti is perhaps
more famous for his work at the Palazzo Pitti and adjoining
Boboli Gardens.

VIEW ACROSS THE ROOFTOPS
Volterra

The magical and beautiful town of Volterra has a rich and
fascinating history that includes the Etruscans, the Romans, the
Florentines and the art treasures of a once flourishing
Renaissance. Each layer of the town's history is visible within its
soft-coloured stone structures, from the surviving parts of the
Etruscan town walls, to the Roman amphitheatre and antiquities,
to the twentieth century satellite dishes that poke randomly from
the tiled rooftops. Surrounding the town are fragments of rocky
crags, *the balze*, a stone ridge on which the old town was built,
and which subsequently started to crumbled.

CAMPANILE
Volterra

The centre of Volterra revolves around the impressive Piazza dei
Priori, which is home to the Palazzo dei Priori, a stunning and
ancient building, and the duomo with its campanile, baptistry
and chapels. The campanile towers above the surrounding
buildings, brilliantly simple in design and powerful in concept.
This is the second bell tower constructed on the site, the
original tower having collapsed; according to an inscription at
its base, the second tower was built in 1493. Although there is
no concrete evidence pertaining to the architect, a very similar
tower was designed by Andrea Sansovino (1460–1529) for the
Sanctuary of Saints George and Christina in Bolsena. Sansovino
also designed the baptismal font at Volterra, and it is possible he
was responsible for the bell tower.

NORTHERN TUSCANY

Northern Tuscany is home to some of the most beautiful scenery, and certainly amongst the most dramatic of Tuscan landscapes. It is a place of striking contrasts from the wild and rugged peaks of the Apuan Alps and the Garfagnana Mountains to the plunging valleys, carved by the crystal waters of the rivers Serchio, Lima, Pescia and their tributaries.

Here the land is rich and fertile, spring-fed and abundant with wildlife; wild flowers grow with tumbling profusion, dark green chestnut trees throw shade, and provide revenue, and rows of ancient olive groves criss-cross the countryside. Northern Tuscany is home too to the famous Carrara marble quarries that appear as brilliant white slices cut into the green mountainsides, to many 'hidden' gem-like villages, small pockets of medieval beauty and the stunning, walled town of Lucca.

In contrast yet again is the coastline of northern Tuscany, a sweep of golden, sand beaches trailing down to the shimmering turquoise Ligurian and Tyrrhenian Seas. This unspoilt area is a jumble of vivid colours, of sea and sand, deckchairs, awnings and dark mountains behind. The many resorts remain, in true Italian style, beautiful and untarnished; places such as Viareggio, whose elegant buildings stand in stately lines, looking out to sea with a whisper of faded extravagance and echoes of its heyday in the late nineteenth and early twentieth century.

VILLA MALASPINA
near Fosdinovo

The elegant Villa Malaspina can be found on the road that
climbs from the village of Caprinola up to the larger town
of Fosdinovo in northern Tuscany, and roughly 110 km
(68 miles) northwest of Florence. It is one of the treasures in
the area, which is often overlooked in the face of the larger
and grander Fosdinovo castle that dominates the scenery
from its hilltop position. The villa was built in 1724 by the
Marquis Gabriele Malaspina on the site of an old tower.
The powerful Malaspina family had held power in the
area since the twelfth century, and the grandeur of this villa
with its beautifully laid out parkland attests to their wealth
and prestige.

MARBLE QUARRIES
near Carrara

The landscape around Carrara gleams with the brilliant white and blue-grey resonance of the local carrara marble. Veins of white slice through the green hillsides, set against the azure of the Mediterranean skies with a striking clash of natural colours. This is the world's most sought after marble, prized by such famous sculptors as Michelangelo (1475–1564) whose statue of David shines white with carrara marble. The area is home to over three hundred quarries, some of which date back to Roman times, and many of which are still in use.

ROCCA
Castiglione di Garfagnana

The village of Castiglione di Garfagnana nestles into the wooded slopes of the Apuan Alps amidst the historic region of Garfagnana in the province of Lucca. It is a beautiful, ancient and fortified place that is dominated by the rustic and mellowed stones of the 'Rocca' or castle. The village, perched on its steep slopes, affords sweeping panoramic views across the breathtaking countryside and is perfectly placed as a defensive post. It was first settled by the Romans and later fell to the Lombards, the Franks and the Luccans; it was the Lords of Lucca who built the Rocca, which dates to 1371.

TOWARDS THE TOWN
Castelnuovo di Garfagnana

The picturesque town of Castelnuovo di Garfagnana spreads along the lush, green Serchio valley, home to the area's third largest river that wends its way from Mount Sillano across the region of Garfagnana and on to the Ligurian Sea. It is a charming and thoroughly unspoilt town that resonates with a quiet sense of history, while its simple and beautiful buildings jostle together in a surprising hotch-potch of narrow, winding streets. Presiding over the town is the imposing twelfth-century fortress, the Rocca Ariostesca, as well as a well-restored sixteenth-century cathedral.

48

SERCHIO VALLEY
The Garfagnana

The Serchio Valley is simply stunning; steep, densely wooded and dark green mountainsides, the Apennine and Alpi Appuane ranges, plunge down to the valley bottom. Dotted along the steep inclines are buildings that cling to the sides, rising up majestic from amidst the chestnut tree groves, chestnut flour once being a primary industry in this agricultural area. It is a landscape of sweeping, sublime beauty with towering, rocky peaks dwarfing the small towns and villages that sit within the valley perimeters. The Serchio Valley is wild, unspoilt and intensely moving, full of natural wonders and architectural delights.

STREET SCENE
Cutigliano

This medieval hill town perches high in the Tuscan-Emilian Appenines in the province of Pistoia, and overlooks the fertile Lima valley. Typically of many Tuscan hillside towns, Cutigliano is a surprising and almost incidental sight with beautiful, mellowed buildings topped by russet roofs rising up from the dense and dark, wooded slopes around it. The town originally developed along an important medieval route, the Alpe alla Croce, that formed the junction between Pistoia and Modena, and retains its authentic medieval atmosphere. The narrow streets are lined with lovely buildings and monuments, with tall trees providing shade and casting long shadows back and forth across the roads.

PARISH CHURCH
Cutigliano

The small and beautiful village of Cutigliano is home to two extraordinary buildings, the Palazzo Pretorio and the Parish Church. The church, sun dappled through the trees, presides at one end of the village, clinging to the steep hillside. Its simple exterior is largely unadorned, but bathed in the sharp Mediterranean sun, glistens with a soft white glow that is visible, set against the dark hillside, from quite some distance. Inside the church are works of art by several Tuscan masters including Giovanni da San Giovanni (1592–1636) who painted the *Circumcision of Jesus* in 1620 to decorate the left wall of the sanctuary.

PALAZZO PRETORIO
Cutigliano

Set in the heart of Cutigliano, a medieval town that still reverberates with a sense of history, is the Palazzo Pretorio. This striking and unusual fourteenth-century palace is perhaps most distinctive through the carved escutcheons that decorate the facade. These beautiful carvings are rich and varied, and include the Medici Pope's coat of arms, and those of many medieval rulers: they have survived the years well, and their details, down even to the inscriptions they bear, are clearly visible. The palazzo was built by the ruling authority of the area, the Capitanato della Montagna, who also controlled other nearby palazzi in an effort to maintain the defensive lines of the area.

CASINO
Bagni di Lucca

The creamy-white and yellow-ochre buildings of Bagni di Lucca line the banks of the fast-moving river Lima, while behind the town a rich, dark green blanket of trees stretches across the surrounding hills. It is an elegant and once opulent town, being one of the most fashionable spa resorts in the nineteenth century. Today echoes of her former grandeur can be felt through the fine architecture, including the Casino, built in 1837 and one of Europe's first licensed gambling houses. In 1805 a new road was built to the town at the insistence of Napoleon Bonaparte's (1769–1821) sister, and it subsequently became a favourite destination for the Bonaparte family.

TORRENTE LIMA
Bagni di Lucca

The Lima valley is a beautiful lush and fertile area through which tumbles the river Lima. Bagni di Lucca is the main town in the valley, and it developed alongside the banks of the turbulent Lima. The hills surrounding the town are full of natural springs, and in Roman times the settlement gained a reputation for its curative spas. The town's prestige has since rested upon its spas through history. During the Middle Ages and the Renaissance, Bagni di Lucca was a fashionable destination, and in the nineteenth century its status as an elegant spa resort reached an apogee.

TEMPIETTO DEMIDOFF
Bagni di Lucca

The striking neoclassical Tempietto Demidoff sits back into the carpeted green hillside, a muted yellow and white structure of infinite harmony. Its neoclassical proportions and simple but elegant exterior lend it an air of quiet and faded grandeur, which is in keeping with much of the character of Bagni di Lucca as a whole. The Tempietto was built at the same time as the Ospedale Demidoff, a fine house and baths, in 1828. They sit between the Ponte a Serraglio, a stone bridge, and Fornoli, a small market village, near Bagni di Lucca, on the Torrente Camaione.

TOWARDS THE VILLAGE
Montefegatesi

Montefegatesi sits perched some 13 km (8 miles) above Bagni di Lucca on the mountainside, and offers breathtaking views down the Lima valley and across the surrounding countryside. It is a tiny, unspoilt hamlet that is far from the beaten trail and is a secret and delightful corner of Tuscany. Close to the village itself are two extraordinary beauty spots, the Orrido di Botri, which is a vertiginous, craggy gorge with a torrential stream at the bottom, and just above Montefegatesi is the Prato Fiorito (Flowery Meadow), which is carpeted with flowers throughout much of the spring.

CHESTNUT WOODS
The Lima Valley

The beautiful Lima valley is home to many small hamlets and villages, and some larger towns, though even these are moderate. These settlements spread along the hillsides of the valley, poking up from amongst the dark, green-forested landscape. Much of the industry in this quiet, beautiful area was based on agriculture, and in particular revolved around the chestnut trees that line the valley sides. These important and magnificent trees have through history kept the small pockets of population going, both through their derivative, chestnut flour, and for firewood. Amongst the locals these trees are occasionally referred to as the 'bread tree', reflecting the fundamental importance they have had to sustaining the communities.

PONTE DELLA MADDALENA
Borgo a Mozzano

The extraordinary Ponte della Maddalena, also sometimes called Ponte del Diavolo (the Devil's Bridge), spans the river Serchio near the town of Borgo a Mozzano. The bridge, which dominates the area, was part of an important trade and pilgrimage route that ran effectively from Rome to France and was known as the Via Francigena. It is first thought to have been commissioned in around 1080–1100, and today represents one of the finest examples of medieval bridge building still in existence. Quite apart from its functional aspect the bridge is beautifully proportioned and fluid in outline. The reflection cast on the waters of the Serchio increase its dynamism and give it the appearance of a mysterious portal.

BEACH AT LIDO DI CAMAIORE
Versilia

The vibrant array of beach umbrellas and deck chairs, flags, balls and boards set against the turquoise sea and azure sky gives this small section of the Tuscan coastline a painterly effect in true Italian style. The municipal district of Camaiore, part of Versilia, sits in a basin with the Apuan Alps towering, dark and broody, behind and the vast expanse of glittering Tyrrhenian Sea stretching out in front. Within the Camaiore district is the small bathing spa town of Lido di Camaiore, a beach town that winds along the shoreline and boosts an elegant promenade with shops and restaurants.

LIBERTY-STYLE SHOP
Viareggio

Viareggio, translated as 'King's Road', is one of the largest and most popular resort destinations along the Versilia coastline, and is particularly notable for its elegant Art Nouveau architecture. The town takes its name from the Via Regis, a long coastal road, which transects the town, dates to medieval times and is still in existence. The town itself was not fully established until the sixteenth century, and from then has steadily grown. In 1917 the timber buildings and boardwalks were destroyed by a fire, and the subsequent Art Nouveau buildings, erected to replace these in 1920, now give the town much of its refined character.

BEACH FRONT
Viareggio

Viareggio's popularity as a beach resort took hold in 1823 when the first bathing establishments were opened, and since then it has become one of the most fashionable holiday destinations along the Versilia coast, even earning the nickname, 'the Pearl of the Tyrrhenian'. Some of Viareggio's more famous guests have included the poets Percy B. Shelley (1792–1822), Lord Byron (1788–1824), Alessandro Manzoni (1785–1873) and Gabriele D'Annunzio (1863–1938) and the composer Giacomo Puccini (1858–1924). The oldest building in the town is the Torre Mathilde (Matilda's Tower), which dates to 1541 and is a defensive fortress built by the Lucchesi.

CARNIVAL OF VIAREGGIO
Viareggio

Every January and February Viareggio hosts its annual carnival, for which the town has now become most famous. Dating back to 1873, the carnival was first staged by a group of wealthy individuals in the weeks before Easter, who decorated floats with flowers and fruit and paraded them through the town. Local residents donned masks in retaliation against the high taxes they were forced to pay. Today people flock to the parade to see the extravagant and creative papier-mâché floats and figures, which are virtually unequalled. The official mascot of the parade is the clown figure, Burlamacco, who was designed by the artist Uberto Bonetti (1909–93) in 1931.

VIEW OF THE CITY
Lucca

Lucca is an ancient and delightful city, the original sector still secreted behind walls built during the Renaissance, and the city plan retaining its Roman roots. The area became a Roman colony in 180 BC, although it had been settled long before this time. The centre of the city is built along the rectangular Roman grid formation; where the original forum once was is now the grand Piazza S. Michele. The walls, which remain intact, were built over a long period of time, and were finished during the seventeenth century.

SAN MICHELE IN FORO
Lucca

This unusual and captivating church sits in the Piazza S. Michele and was built slowly between the eleventh and fourteenth century. The facade, with its wonderful twisted columns, each one different, and carved marble details is an extravagant example of the Pisan-Romanesque style. One of the most striking aspects of this church's decoration is the lack of obvious Christian detailing, with a few exceptions, one being the large winged figure of St Michael on the pediment, which alludes to the building's Christian purpose. Perhaps unsurprisingly, until 1370 the Church was originally used as the assembly halls for the seat of the *Consiglio Maggiore* (Major Council).

ANFITEATRO ROMANO
Lucca

On first glance the Piazza Anfiteatro Romano appears to be an expansive and grand piazza, which is not unusual in such a city. On further inspection, however, the shape of the piazza suddenly becomes clear, revealing the old structure of the Roman amphitheatre. At one end of the piazza low archways mark the points where gates once would have stood, to allow wild animals and gladiators into the arena. Over time the original stones of the structure were removed and used in other buildings in the town, in the churches and the walls in particular. Today the amphitheatre is lined with elegant buildings painted in subtle and engaging colours, and bathed in the brilliant Tuscan sunlight.

TORRE DEI GUINIGI
Lucca

This extraordinary tower, topped with several holm oak trees sprouting like wild-kept hair, forms part of the Case Guinigi, and is the only remaining tower from the original four. The Guinigi were a powerful family who lived in Lucca, with Paolo Guinigi ruling the city for the first part of the fifteenth century. The house and adjoining towers, which represent one of the most interesting examples of medieval architecture in Lucca, were begun in 1384 and built from brick, sandstone from Matraia, and Verrucano from the Monti Pisani. This remaining tower stands 44.25 m (145 ft) high and, along with the imposing house, would have been a clear symbol of the Guinigi's power and wealth.

SAN MARTINO DUOMO
Lucca

The oldest part of the cathedral dates back to the sixth century, although much of it was rebuilt in the eleventh century by Pope Alexander II (d. 1073). The building was further added to and extended over succeeding centuries, with the west front being built in 1204 and the beautiful Gothic nave and transepts in the fourteenth century. The cathedral houses many artefacts and works of art, but its most precious is an ancient wooden crucifix bearing an image of Christ wearing a long, sleeveless garment. The crucifix is alleged to have been carved by Christ's contemporary, Nicodemus, who was benevolent towards him, and who appears several times in the Gospel.

CHURCH OF SAN FREDANIO
Lucca

The striking Romanesque church of San Fredanio dominates one
end of the Piazza San Fredanio, and is imposing, grand and a little
overbearing. The monumentality of its plain facade is alleviated by
the stunning thirteenth-century mosaic, which glows brilliantly
with gold, vibrant blue and pale pinks and pastels. The church
itself was begun in the sixth century and commissioned by
Fredanio, Bishop of Lucca, who dedicated it to St Vincent. When
Fredanio died he was buried in the church, and it was renamed
in his honour. Between 1112 and 1147 the building was turned
into the Romanesque form now apparent, with the mosaic of
The Ascension of Christ the Saviour being added later.

STREET SCENE
Collodi

Collodi is a small village that stretches in a narrow ribbon
(often no more than several houses wide) up the side of a steep
Tuscan hill not far from the larger town of Pescia. At the top of
the beautifully preserved medieval village is the thirteenth-
century church of San Bartolomeo, filled with fifteenth-century
frescos, while at the bottom of the small hamlet is the striking
Villa Garzoni with its magnificent baroque gardens. Many of
Collodi's narrow streets are stepped, such is the village's
gradient, and the soft coloured stone houses throw deep
shadows along their length.

GARDENS OF VILLA GARZONI
Collodi

The impressive Villa Garzoni with her spectacular gardens can
be found at the bottom end of the small, ancient, medieval
town of Collodi. The villa, which is on a monumental scale, was
built for Ramono Garzoni, a member of the powerful Garzoni
family, and was to replace their earlier and much damaged
castle. The villa was built in the Luccan Baroque style between
1633 and 1662, while the gardens as they appear today were not
designed until 1786. Their plan is largely symmetrical and, due
to the geography of the land, much of them are stepped or
terraced. Of particular note is the lavishly ornate baroque
terrace feature, pictured, which includes complicated carved
patterned details and statuary.

PINOCCHIO PARK
Collodi

Apart from her historic architecture and beauty, Collodi is
also famous for the character Pinocchio, created by the writer
Carol Lorenzini (1826–90). Lorenzini, who wrote under the
pen name Carlo Collodi, grew up in the Villa Garzoni, where
his mother had been born, and whose magical gardens may
have provided the author with some of his inpsiration.
The Pinocchio Park was opened in 1956 in his memory, and
is filled with sculptures, installations and exhibitions set amidst
gorgeous landscape and dedicated to the story of the little
wooden puppet with the long nose.

TOWARDS THE TOWN
Uzzano

The hilltop town of Uzzano enjoys staggering views of the
surrounding valleys, green and carpeted richly with a profusion
of wild flowers, and gnarled olive groves. The valleys are fed by
springs from the river Pescia, and are extremely lush and fertile.
The small town's location was ideal in defensive terms with its
panoramic views, and is entered through a narrow, stone
archway. It was first settled during the sixth or seventh century
by the Germanic Lombards, but is not mentioned until AD
1000 when it had come under Luccan power. Today the pale-
coloured buildings cluster together, and are presided over by the
parish church of Saints Jacopo and Martino, as well as the
magnificent Palazzo del Capitano del Popolo.

PALAZZO DEL CAPITANO DEL POPOLO
Uzzano

After passing through the narrow, stone entry gateway into the
ancient town of Uzzano, there stretches before you the
charming Piazza Umberto, from which there are breathtaking
views of the Pescia valley. Located within this central piazza is
the imposing Palazzo del Capitano del Popolo (Captain of the
People), which was first begun in the fourteenth century and
was subsequently much added to. The attractive open loggia of
the palazzo provides shade for the local townsfolk, and a place
for people to gather out of the sharp Mediterranean sun.

PIAZZA DEL DUOMO
Prato

The bustling city of Prato has been the centre of Italy's
textile industry since the Middle Ages, and still produces
almost three-quarters of Italy's wool. The city is home to the
striking Cathedral of St Stephen, which can be found in the
expansive Piazza del Duomo. The cathedral has a particularly
beautiful International Gothic style facade (added in the early
fifteenth century), and is also one of the city's oldest religious
buildings, dating back to the tenth century. It is home to an
important collection of artefacts and paintings including the
Sacra Cintola (Belt of the Holy Virgin) and Fra Filippo Lippi's
(1406–69) beautiful *Life of John the Baptist* 1452–66.

EASTERN TUSCANY

On the western sides of the Apennines and stretching to the east towards the border with Umbria is an area of Tuscany that is rich in culture and heritage. This is eastern Tuscany, which is largely comprised of the province of Arezzo, named after the main city in the area.

Once the city of Arezzo rivalled Florence in terms of power and wealth and, along with Perugia and Siena, was one of the dominant and warring factions, with Tuscany's smaller towns and villages falling first to one power and then the next. These battles have been laid to rest and today Arezzo, a little faded, plasterwork slightly crumbled, is instead a thriving centre of arts and culture; birthplace of both the humanist Petrarch (1304–74) and Giorgio Vasari (1511–74), and home to one of the most striking collections of Piero della Francesca's (c. 1412–92) art works.

Spreading across part of the Apennines is the Casentino Forest, a dense and dark sward of silver firs, beech and chestnut trees, and dotted in amongst the canopy are small villages, russet roof tops just visible between the trees. The Camaldoli Monastery perches here, commanding stunning views across the forest and beyond, while the ancient medieval villages of Stia and Poppi are dotted along the Arno river valley far below. River valleys dominate in this part of Tuscany, carved out by the Arno and the great Tiber that wends its way to Rome, as well as the smaller though equally beautiful Esse river valley and the Chiani.

PALAZZO DEI VICARI
Scarperia

The small town of Scarperia can be found approximately 25 km (15.5 miles) northeast of Florence, and is situated on what was once the main trade route between Florence and Bologna. The town was founded by the Florentines in 1306, and was built as a defensive settlement against marauders from the north. That same year the architect Arnolfo di Cambio (*c.* 1232–*c.* 1310) was commissioned to build the stunning Palazzo dei Vicari, one of the most striking buildings in Scarperia. In subsequent years noblemen added their family coat of arms to the building's exterior, which is today covered in a fascinating collection of them.

TRADITIONAL METALWARE FATTORIA
Scarperia

During the fifteenth and sixteenth century many workshops opened up in Scarperia, and in particular metalworking businesses. Much of the town's economy later revolved around its metalwork, and it became famous for its wrought iron and cutlery, especially knives. In 1908 the production of knives was slowed by a law prohibiting the trade and use of pocket knives longer than a palm's length. In more recent years the age-old tradition of metalwork has been re-established in the town, and workshops have opened up again.

PIAZZA GIOTTO
Vicchio

Vicchio is one of the most elegant small towns in Eastern
Tuscany, its sunlit streets lined with perfectly proportioned,
grand buildings in an array of architectural styles. The town is
reached via a simple bridge that spans the river Sieve, and
was first settled by the Etruscans. It is a place linked with
famous artists, including Giotto (*c.* 1267–1337), whose bronze
statue by Italo Vagnetti (1864–1933), presides magnificently
over the Piazza Giotto, as well as the artist Fra Angelico
(*c.* 1395–1455) and his brother Benedetto. Vicchio is also
home to an impressive collection of works of art in its
Museo Civico Beato Angelico.

GIOTTO'S HOUSE AT VESPIGNANO
near Vicchio

The famous fourteenth century painter Giotto di Bondone was born just a short distance from the town of Vicchio in Vespignano. His house has since been preserved and turned into a museum documenting his life, and full of reproductions of his exquisite works of art. The shaded building, which nestles beneath tall, fragrant trees, sits on the beautiful Vespignano hillside, just below the church of San Martino. Built in medieval times, the house has been added to, and suffered damage over the centuries. It was only fully restored in 1977, having for some time been used as a farm outbuilding.

MEDICI VILLA DI CAFAGGIOLO
near Vicchio

Standing imposing, striking and brilliant against the backdrop of Tuscan hills is the Medici Villa di Cafaggiolo, with its surrounding flower-filled meadows sloping down to the river Sieve. The building has been greatly added to and changed, particularly during the nineteenth century, but its quintessential Renaissance core is still clearly visible. It was built in 1451 by Michelozzo Michelozzi (1396–1472) for the Medici family, and became the favourite residence of Lorenzo the Magnificent (1449–92). Michelozzi created the palace on the site of a former manor house, and turned it into an opulent and impressive country estate reflective of the Medici's great power and wealth.

CAPELLINA DELLA BRUNA
near *Vicchio*

This tiny chapel stands in magnificent isolation in the
sweeping fields just beyond the town of Vicchio, and not far
from Giotto's house. The building is dwarfed by cypress trees,
which encircle it, and by the sheer expanse of landscape itself
that stretches back towards the distant Tuscan hills. The
building is ancient, and simple in design; a tiny corner of
religious intent in a wide-open countryside. It was dedicated
to the blessed Giovanni de' Bruni, who was born in
Vespignano in 1234, and who is reputed to have prayed
there, and contains a somewhat damaged fresco attributed to
Paolo Schiavo (1397–1478) or his school.

MONASTERY
Camaldoli

The ancient monastic village of Camaldoli sits in a remote
corner of the Casentino forest, which spreads across part of the
Apennine Mountains. Reached via a twisted mountain road, the
monastery affords the most spectacular views across the
countryside, in every direction, and is at once both exhilarating
and humbling. The monastery was founded in 1012 by St
Romuald, a former hermit, who set about to combine aspects
of monastic and hermitic life through Camaldoli. It was
originally a starkly simple building that was later greatly
expanded and embellished, particularly in 1658 and 1693. Today
the monastery is characterized by its lavish baroque facade,
striking towers, and impressive collection of art works.

TOWARDS THE VILLAGE
Stia

Stia is a true gem of a tiny village, whose heart and vitality
belies its diminutive size. The buildings cluster together at the
point where the river Staggia meets the great river Arno,
while behind the village rises the stunning Monte Falterona.
Much of Stia's industry has revolved around the wool trade, the
waters of her rivers being particularly suited to processing wool,
and wrought iron work. As with so many Tuscan villages her
walls conceal a surprisingly rich collection of art works
including pieces by the Della Robbia family and Bicci di
Lorenzo (1373–1452).

WEST TOWARDS FLORENCE
Stia

The area surrounding the small village of Stia is lush, fertile
and spring-fed. Almost as far as the eye can see spread the
familiar rows of vineyards, patchworking the countryside, and
olive groves ripe with fruit. In the distance the mountains
loom grey-blue through the hazy Mediterranean sun with
Florence, the artistic heart of Tuscany, hovering some 50 km
(31 miles) away. Stia itself boasts a lively market centred
around the main Piazza Tanucci, which is dominated by an
unusual and striking fountain. Every two years the village
hosts the Mostra d'Arte Fabbrile, a large exhibition of
traditional crafts, including quilts, woollen garments and
wrought iron works.

TOWARDS THE CASENTINO VALLEY
Poppi

The beautiful, small town of Poppi can be found between
Florence and Arrezzo, nestled into the vibrantly green and lush
valley of the river Arno. The town, which is medieval in
character, is full of narrow streets lined by tall, majestic
buildings, that open suddenly and unexpectedly into charming,
light-filled piazzas; it is full of the contrasts of muted shadows
and brilliant light. Dominating the town is the imposing
Castello degli Conti Guidi, which contains an impressive
library, art collection and chapel, and also the twelfth century
Church of San Fedele.

CASTELLO DEGLI CONTI GUIDI
Poppi

The heavily fortified Castello degli Conti Guidi presides over
the town of Poppi, which rests in the upper reaches of the Arno
river valley. Set on the top of a small hill, the castle is both
moated and surrounded by battlement walls, largely devoid of
windows on the lower sections and leaving no doubt as to the
defensive purpose of this building. To one side rises the castle's
tower, which is starkly simple but impressively grand. This was
the seat of the Guidi family who first ruled the valley from
approximately 1000 to 1289 when it fell to the Florentines, and
then continued to live in the Castello until 1448.

MICHELANGELO MUSEUM
Caprese Michelangelo

Caprese Michelangelo is truly a hidden and glorious
corner of Tuscany, often overlooked in the face of its more
famous and prestigious relatives, but one not to be missed.
The village takes its name from the Latin word '*capra*' or
wild goat, which are not uncommon in the area, and from
the famous artist Michelangelo Buonarroti (1475–1564).
In 1875 a copy of Michelangelo's birth certificate, signed
by his father, was uncovered and named Caprese as his
birthplace, finally ending a dispute between the village of
Caprese and Chiusi della Verna who had also proclaimed
itself as his birthplace.

VIEW OF THE TOWN
Anghiari

The strongly fortified medieval town of Anghiari rests between two great rivers, the Tiber and the Arno, and overlooks the gorgeous Tiber valley. The Romans first settled the area, then later in the thirteenth century the defensive walls were added to encircle and protect the town. It is famous for the Battle of Anghiari, which took place on June 29, 1440 and saw the Florentines reassert their power over the area. The battle scene was painted by Leonardo da Vinci (1452–1519) in 1505 for the walls of the Palazzo Vecchio in Florence, though was later 'lost' after the palace was remodelled by Giorgio Vasari (1511–74).

TOWARDS THE TOWN
Monterchi

The town of Monterchi sits atop a small hill in the Cerfone valley; a tiny patch of buildings all jumbled together and encircled by fortified medieval stone walls. In Etruscan and Roman times the area was referred to as Hercules' Hill, and was home to a cult worshipping the ancient God. It was a place with strong pagan attachments, which included the belief that the local spring water had fertility properties and was beneficial for barren women. Today Monterchi is perhaps most famous for being the birthplace of Piero della Francesca's (*c.* 1412–92) mother, and is home to his exquisite *Madonna del Parto* (the Madonna of Childbirth), 1445.

TOWARDS THE CERFONE VALLEY
Monterchi

The views from Monterchi across the Cerfone Valley to the hills
beyond are quite stunning, with receding patchwork fields of
crops crossed by dark lines of trees. It is an area of great beauty,
a small pocket in the west of the Arezzo province that borders
on to Umbria, and produces some fine wines. It was first ruled
by the marquises of Santa Maria, before the Tarlati family came
to power. The Tarlatis built an impressive castle just beyond the
town, which was later turned into a convent and then mostly
destroyed in 1643, leaving just remnants of the walls.

DUOMO
Arezzo

The large city of Arezzo has ancient roots and was one of the
primary settlements for the Etruscans; its history as a substantial
centre of trade and commerce is therefore a long and rich one.
The city stretches across a steep incline on the side of the Arno
valley and is home to a vast number of historically and artistically
important churches. In the midst of these is the magnificent
duomo, which was built on the highest elevation in the city, and
on the site of an earlier Benedictine chapel. The cathedral was
begun in 1277, with work continuing sporadically through the
years right up to the twentieth century. It houses numerous works
of art including Piero della Francesca's fresco, *Magdalene*, 1459.

LOGGIA RISTORANTE
Arezzo

The town has a rich and vibrant mix of ancient and modern, of architectural gems and works of art nudging alongside a cosmopolitan and fast-paced city. It is full of elegant shops and restaurants, some secreted beneath magnificent loggias, the lofty arches and substantial columns dwarfing the bright white squares of tables and inviting wicker chairs. The sense of history in Arezzo is present at every turn, and its centre has remained remarkably medieval in character, in particular the Piazza Grande, which was once the centre of commercial activity.

TOWARDS THE TOWN
Monte San Savino

Shimmering against the distant horizon is the town of Monte San Savino, its skyline distinguished by its three belfries, one being square in design, one domed and one pointed. The town sits on a hill that dominates the surrounding Esse river valley and has stunning views across the surrounding landscape. Through the middle of the town runs the Corso Sangallo, an ancient thoroughfare, which is lined with monuments on either side, including those by the artist Andrea Sansovino (*c.* 1467–1529) who was born there. For a small town, Monte San Savino is home to a large number of particularly fine palazzos, including the Renaissance Palazzo della Cancelleria and the High Renaissance Palazzo di Monte.

PORTA FIORENTINA
Monte San Savino

The history of Monte San Savino is one filled with incessant power struggles that saw the town repeatedly taken over, by the Florentines, by Perugia, Arezzo and Siena. Every ruling faction left their mark in some way upon the town, but perhaps most reflective of its troubled past is the fortified nature of the place. A defensive wall surrounds the town with four entrance gateways carved within its sloping sides. The most impressive of these is the Porta Fiorentina, which was carved by Giorgio Vasari in 1550 and has Cosimo de' Medici's coat of arms set prominently above it.

TOWARDS THE TOWN
Lucignano

Seen from a distance the strategic placement of Lucignano on the top of a small hill is most apparent, and was of supreme importance to the little town that was constantly involved in power struggles. It is situated along the main pass between Siena and Arezzo, overlooking the valley of Chiana, and is one of the most interesting and best-preserved medieval towns. Its plan is elliptical, with streets running in concentric rings towards the middle, and protected along the outer edge by a fortified wall. The rich and poor areas of the town were divided by roads; the Borgo Ricco (now Via Matteotti) being lined with elegant grand buildings for the rich, while smaller houses for the poorer inhabitants could be found along the Via Corsica (now Via Roma) and to the north.

ROCCA
Lucignano

The impressive and impregnable tower, part of the fourteenth
century fortress that presides over Lucignano's muted terracotta
roofs is a surviving reminder of the town's constant defensive
action as it was taken over alternately by Siena, Arezzo, Florence
and Perugia. The town still retains Perugia's coat of arms of a
winged griffon, and an added star to denote its hilltop position.
The layout of the town as it appears today was developed in the
thirteenth century, and the fortifications in the town, the walls
and the three gates were finished in 1371, while Lucignano was
under Siena's rule.

CHURCH OF SAN FRANCISCO
Lucignano

Set amidst the curving streets of Lucignano, with their tall, ochre
houses and colourful shutters, is a surprising number of impressive
buildings, churches tucked away and palazzos. The Gothic Chiesa
San Francisco is just one example, whose striking Romanesque
facade decorated with horizontal bands of dark brick is utterly
unexpected, and dwarfed by the Palazzo Communale that sits
further along in the piazza. The Chiesa dates back to 1248,
and houses a number of exquisite frescos by Bartolo di Fredi
(*c.* 1330–1410) and Taddeo di Bartolo (*c.* 1362–1422). No less
unexpected is the astonishing baroque high altar designed in
1709 by Andrea Pozzo (1642–1709) and concealed within
Lucignano's Collegiate Church of San Michele.

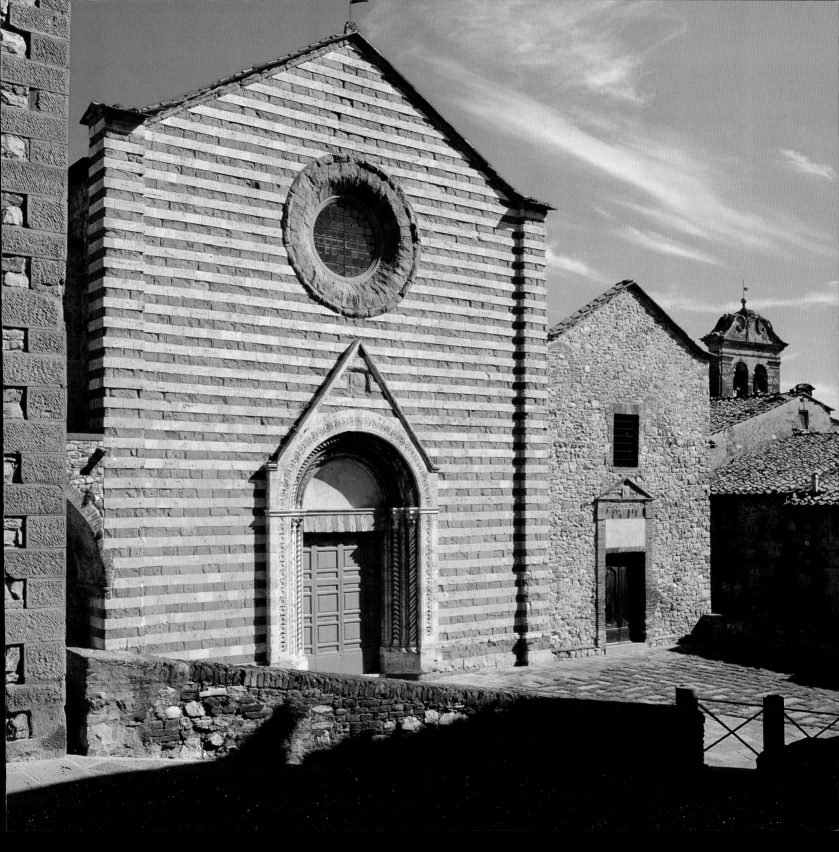

TOWARDS THE TOWN
Foiano della Chiana

The small mostly medieval town of Foiano della Chiana sits on
a small hill between the fertile Chiana and Esse river valleys.
The settlement dates back to Roman times, and possibly before,
but the core of the town was built during the Middle Ages, and
much of its medieval character remains. The streets weave their
way back and forth across the hillside in a jumble of narrow
roads that open suddenly into beautiful light-bathed squares,
or turn into steeply stepped passageways, which twist their
way to the top of the town. At every turn the buildings have
faded from hundreds of years of bright sunlight to the
mellowed, soft colours that are typical of Tuscany.

ART INSIDE THE COLLEGIATA
Foiano della Chiana

The Corso Vittorio Emanuele, an elegant street, leads to the
open Piazza della Collegiata, which is home to the impressive
Collegiate church of San Martino. The church, with its
striking baroque facade, was begun in 1512, but not finished
until 1796. Within its stone walls are a number of important
art works, including the *Madonna della Cintola*, 1502, by
Andrea della Robbia (1435–1525) and the *Coronation of the
Virgin* (pictured here), by Luca Signorelli (*c.* 1445–1523) and his
school. The *Coronation of the Virgin* was one of Signorelli's last
works, and was painted by the elderly artist (and his pupils) after
he had become partially paralysed.

PANORAMA OF THE TOWN
Cortona

Cortona is one of Tuscany's oldest hill towns and was first settled by the Etruscans. The area is rich in Etruscan artefacts as well as tombs, and many of these findings are now on display at the comprehensive Museo dell'Accademia Etrusca in the Palazzo Casali. The settlement grew along the slopes of Monte Sant' Egidio, with steeply inclined streets and terraced banks of houses protected behind the smooth, defensive walls. From the top of the town there are breathtaking views across the Chiana river valley to the distant blue haze of the Siena Mountains, and the flat, mirror surface of the impressive Trasimeno lake.

TOWN STREET AND FOUNTAIN
Cortona

Although settled by the Etruscans, the prevailing character of
Cortona is medieval, and her streets are lined with slightly
crumbling but exquisite examples of architecture from this
period. The town is enclosed by walls, which were built on top
of the existing remains of the Etruscan walls, and her streets
beyond wind their way, narrow and shaded, leading to open
piazzas. At her heart Cortona is a town of art works, sculptures
and fountains. She was the birthplace of the artists Luca
Signorelli and Pietro Berrettini, known as Pietro da Cortona,
(1596–1669) and, much later, Gino Severini (1883–1966).

CHURCH OF
SANTA MARIA DELLE GRAZIE
Cortona

As with so many Italian towns, Cortona is home to a surprising
number of beautiful churches, which contain exquisite works of
art. The church of Santa Maria delle Grazie can be found to the
edge of the town, her impressive dome punctuating the skyline
above the terracotta tiled roofs below. The church was built by
Francesco di Giorgio Martini (1439–1502), begun in 1484 and
finished posthumously in 1515, and is a beautiful example of
Renaissance church design. Although its exterior is simple with
its plain facade and harmonious proportions, the interior is of
particular note, and has been carefully restored.

CENTRAL TUSCANY

Central Tuscany has its own unique character that is quite different in feel from other parts of the region. It is overwhelmingly rural and, although the heart of Tuscany in geographical terms, it is perhaps the quietest patch, full of tiny hidden hamlets that spring suddenly to view with a passing bend in the road, and long fields of vines and olives heavily laden with fruit.

Unlike the dramatic landscape of northern or eastern Tuscany, this area is one of gently rolling hills, peculiarly and distinctively conical and most often surmounted by ancient fortified villages; there are wide reaches of flat, fertile plains and smoothly-flowing rivers wend their way politely through the countryside.

Throughout the Middle Ages and beyond, the country that sweeps from Florence to Siena has rung with the battle cries of both cities as they fought over the land and the small, fortified towns in between. This area is Chianti, most famous now for its wine production. The scenery here is a patchwork of vineyards that jostle up against ancient olive groves and dark cypress trees, and spread across the undulating landscape. Siena, central Tuscany's capital and jewel, sits to the south of the province, a city rich in art and culture. To the south and east of Siena, Crete Senesi is revealed, a landscape often painted by artists of the Renaissance, with its characteristic grey, clay soil and web of river valleys including those of the Arbia, Asso and Ombrone, while running from the south of Siena to the chestnut-wooded eastern slopes of Monte Amiata is the breathtaking Val d'Orcia.

TOWARDS THE TOWN
San Gimignano

Most striking about San Gimignano seen from a distance is its skyline punctuated with towers; it is also referred to as the 'Town of the Beautiful Towers'. There were at one time as many as seventy towers in the medieval town, although today only thirteen remain. Powerful local families built them during the Middle Ages as defensive structures; they provided an excellent view across the landscape to spot marauders, as well as being virtually impregnable. San Gimignano was first settled by the Etruscans in the third century BC, although its buildings and plan based around two major streets with four main piazzas was not established until the Middle Ages.

CAMPANILE
San Gimignano

From the mellowed stones of the campanile, or bell tower, there is a tantalizing view across the surrounding countryside, which is of particular beauty. The area around San Gimignano is renowned for its vineyards and wines, especially the local Vernaccia di San Gimignano, a white wine that has been produced there since 1276, according to records. The sandstone-based soil of the vineyards around San Gimignano suits the Vernaccia grape, which can be difficult to cultivate, and gives the wine its distinctive dry and sharp taste. Dotted amongst the vineyards are the ubiquitous cypress trees, dark and majestic, which also thrive in this area.

TUSCAN VINEYARD
Chianti Region

At the very heart of Tuscany is the region of Chianti, which stretches from Siena to Florence. This beautiful piece of country is famous for its vineyards, which criss-cross the landscape in neat geometric rows, divided by tall, dark cypress trees and with large expanses of flower-filled meadow in between. Chianti wine is one of Italy's most famous, and is a predominantly red wine that was traditionally sold in bulbous bottles with a raffia covering. Although wine has been made in the area for centuries, Chianti as a province of winemaking was not defined until 1716, and in 1932 the area boundaries were extended.

VILLA VIGNAMAGGIO
Greve in Chianti

Greve in Chianti is a small village found on the Florence to Siena route. During the course of its history, and due to its central location, it became an important market place for the numerous palazzos and villas in the surrounding countryside. To the south of Greve and down a tiny winding road is the Villa Vignamaggio, a beautiful, dusky pink building with views across the surrounding olive groves and cypress trees. The house, which has an ornate and formal garden laid out behind, is famous as allegedly being the birthplace of Mona Lisa Gherardini, who later became Lisa del Giocondo, and is reputed to have been Leonardo da Vinci's (1452–1519) model for his painting of the Mona Lisa (1503–06).

PIEVE DI SAN LEOLINO
Panzano in Chianti

The tiny village of Panzano, deep in the heart of Chianti, grew up in the eleventh century around its castle, which sits on a strategic ridge that divides the Val di Greve from the Val di Pesa. Despite its small size, the charming village is home to a number of lovely churches, including the Pieve di San Leolino, the parish church. The original church was built in the eight century, but was completely rebuilt in its present form in the twelfth century and is a fine example of Romanesque architecture. Within the church are two glazed tabernacles attributed to Giovanni della Robbia (1469–*c.* 1529) and an exquisite thirteenth century altar piece by Meliore di Jacopo (*fl. c.* 1260–71).

GOLDEN HAYFIELD
Chianti Region

Chianti is most famous for its vineyards and olive groves that stretch across its gently undulating landscape, but its agricultural industries are varied. The country is particularly fertile, which suits a wide range of crop varieties, but it still comes as something of a surprise when happening upon golden fields of hay after weaving through acres of leafy vines. Dotted through this pastoral piece of Tuscany are numerous small and ancient villages, magnificent Renaissance palazzos and many striking churches. It is an area rich in history, culture and agriculture that has remained unspoilt and relatively unpopulated.

TOWARDS THE TOWN
Radda in Chianti

This little town sits on the top of a small hill that separates the Pesa and Arbia valleys, and lies almost directly on the boundaries of the old Florentine and Sienese territories. This led to Radda being in constant conflict as both factions fought over it. Surrounding the town, and almost as far as the eye can see, are carefully planted vineyards. It remains one of the most prolific wine centres of the region, with the headquarters of the Chianti Classico consortium and the Centro di Studi Chiantigiani (Chianti Studies Centre) located just beyond the town.

CHURCH OF SAN BARNABAS
Castellina in Chianti

The village of Castellina in Chianti was first settled by the
Etruscans and the area is rich in Etruscan artefacts, as well as the
impressive tomb of Montecalvario. Later the village was walled
with just two gates, one facing Florence and one Siena,
although sadly these and much of the walls have since been
destroyed. In the middle of Castellina is the impressive neo–
Romanesque church of San Barnabas built after the original
parish church was destroyed during the Second World War. St
Barnabas is one of the two patron saints of Castellina, and a
Renaissance wood carving of him is kept within the church.

VIA FERRUCCIO
Castellina in Chianti

Castellina is in a particularly strategic position, being on
the top of a small hill, and between the territories of Florence
and Siena. From its position it held sway over the surrounding
web of roads and virtually the entire Elsa river valley. In
the thirteenth century the town became part of the Chianti
Alliance, which was an administrative and military alliance
with Florence, and as such it became a strongly fortified and
defensive settlement. The Via Ferruccio is an important street
within the town and is lined by the Palazzo Ugolini and
the Palazzo Biancardi.

TOWARDS THE TOWN
Monteriggioni

Striking against the horizon is the fortress-like town of
Monteriggioni, which rises from its small hillock position
into the sky with a defiant aspect. This is one of the best-
preserved ancient walled towns in Tuscany, and is still
completely encircled by its formidable defences, which date
to the thirteenth century. Within the walls are fourteen
fortified towers built to defend the town on the northern
borders of Siena's territory against the Florentines. The town
made such an impression on Dante Alighieri (1265–1321)
that he mentioned it in his *Divine Comedy: Inferno* (1308–21).

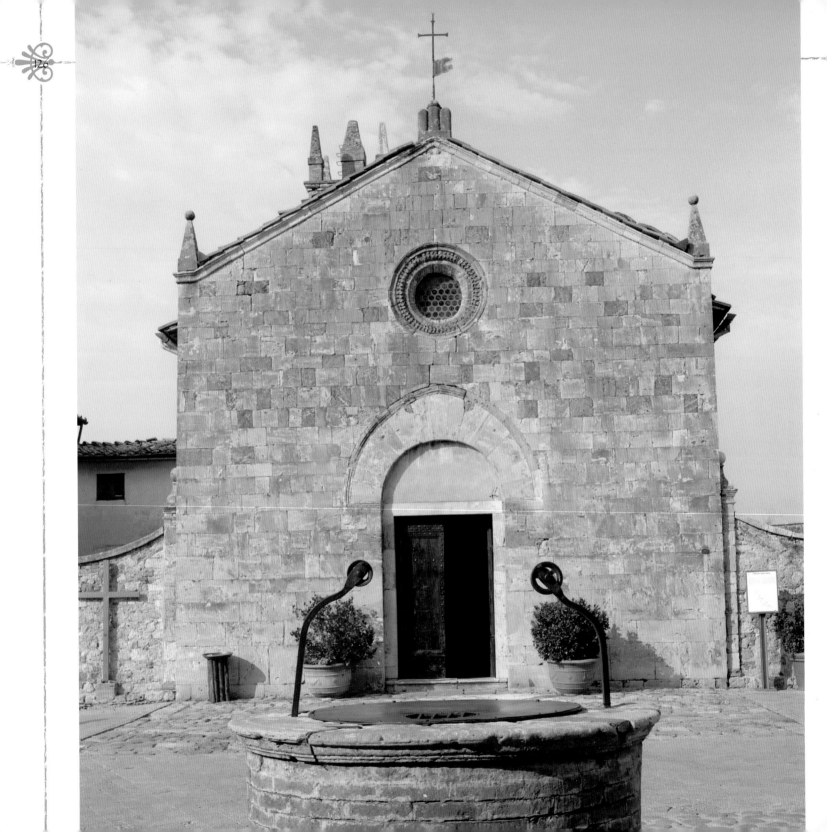

PARISH CHURCH
Monteriggioni

The town of Monteriggioni is small and completely contained within its fortified walls. The central focal point of the town is the main piazza, the Piazza Roma: a beautiful, open space lined with ancient houses and presided over by the parish church. This simple Romanesque-Gothic style church is somewhat defensive in aspect, and reflects the nature of the town. From the Piazza Roma spreads a network of small streets that wind towards the walls and open into public gardens. The gardens were particularly important during times of siege, and were cultivated to feed the town's population.

CLOISTER OF THE CANONICA
Casole d'Elsa

Casole d'Elsa is yet another quiet corner of Tuscany that is far from the beaten trail, and whose buildings conceal a long and at times tumultuous history. Little of the rebellions of her past are discernible, however, when wandering through the often-deserted and tranquil streets and buildings. The cloisters of the Canonica in the Church of Santa Maria Assunta with their beautiful proportions and play of light and shadow are a welcome refuge from the baking Mediterranean sun, and inspire a sense of reflection, while the grand La Rocca, the seat of the Town Hall, imposes its importance, making the passer-by a diminutive detail to the scene.

DUOMO
Siena

Siena, the capital of the province of Siena and the largest city in central Tuscany stretching below Florence, is an architectural, artistic and historical treasure. In the southeast of the city is the spectacular duomo, one of the finest examples of Italian Romanesque-Gothic architecture and one of Italy's most stunning cathedrals. The building, with its distinctive exterior patterned with horizontal bands, was begun in 1136. The facade was finished in 1380, but the extravagant fourteenth century plans to create an extended nave were never completed. Had they been, the duomo would have become the largest church in the Christian world.

PIAZZA DEL CAMPO
Siena

At the centre of the city is the beautiful and magnificent Piazza del Campo, a fan-shaped open space that occupies the site of the former Roman forum. This is truly the heart of Siena, and was for many centuries the primary market place. It is still used as a focal point for festivals and gatherings. The design of the piazza is distinctive and symbolic. The red brick paving is divided into nine segments, which represent the Council of Nine, Siena's ruling body, who commissioned the Piazza in 1293, and also alludes to the nine folds of the Madonna's cloak.

PALAZZO PUBBLICO AND TORRE DEL MANGIA
Siena

Dominating the Piazza del Campo is the magnificent Palazzo Pubblico, Siena's Gothic town hall, with its Torre del Mangia, the bell tower, which is the second tallest medieval tower in Italy. The tower defines Siena's skyline and can be seen from many miles away, rising distinctively above the surrounding buildings like a guardian figure. It was built by two brothers, Muccio and Francesco di Rinaldo between 1138 and 1148, and is an incredible 100 m (330 ft) tall. The Palazzo Pubblico, begun in 1297, is a beautiful example of medieval architecture, and is subtly curved to match the shape of the Piazza del Campo.

PALIO FESTIVAL
Siena

This is Tuscany's most famous festival, which dates back to 1283, but possibly even before this to Roman times. It takes place on 2 July and 2 August each year. The event involves a horse race, which takes place around the perimeter of the Piazza del Campo, with the jockeys representing each of Siena's seventeen districts. The horses are ridden bareback and are drawn by lots, then blessed before the race. There is enormous rivalry between the contestants and each district is fiercely supported by its residents. Surrounding the race dates are several days of festivities, banquets, celebrations and pageantry.

TUSCAN FARMHOUSE
Crete Senesi

The area of Crete Senesi is particularly unique, and can be found to the southeast of Siena stretching through the valleys of the rivers Arbia, Asso and Ombrone. It is the soil, a distinctive grey clay, that lends the area its character, turning the ground a peculiar muted grey. The landscape comprises rolling hills and densely wooded patches, a contrasting and quite striking combination of expansive pastures and tree-covered ribbons. The cypress trees that are such a familiar sight in Tuscany thrive here, delineating property lines and perched in a soldierly fashion along the crests of small hills.

FIELD OF SUNFLOWERS
Val d'Orcia

There is a unique and breathtaking piece of countryside that runs from south of Siena to Monte Amiata. This is Val d'Orcia, possibly one of Tuscany's most famous areas, and one which appears in the background of Renaissance art works with great frequency. Val d'Orcia is characterized by its flat chalk plains, from which rise small, conical hills, many of which have fortified medieval settlements on top. This pastoral area epitomizes the Renaissance ideal of well-managed and aesthetic agricultural countryside, and remains very similar in appearance to the way it was during the fourteenth century.

CISTERCIAN ABBEY
San Galgano

The inspiring beauty of San Galgano and its sense of mystery is quite palatable, and heightened through its ruined state; it is one of the most important religious monuments in Tuscany and is a striking example of Gothic church architecture. It was begun in 1218 near to the small chapel of Monte Siepi to facilitate the increasing numbers of pilgrims travelling to the area. Buried in Monte Siepi are the remains of Saint Galgano, whose legend is closely related to that of King Arthur, down even to the sword buried in a stone, which can also be seen in the chapel.

ROCCA
Montalcino

The small town of Montalcino is perched on the top of a steep hill, with acres of olive groves and vineyards stretching out before it. The heavily fortified town rests behind defensive walls and under the cover of an imposing fourteenth-century fortress topped with tall lookout towers and built in 1361 to a pentagonal plan. Today the fortress's function is rather less aggressive, and the building serves as a wine museum. The area surrounding the town, which is home to excellent examples of thirteenth, fourteenth and fifteenth century architecture, is famous for its production of the Brunello di Montalcino wine.

ABBEY CHURCH OF SANT'ANTIMO
near Montalcino

Not far from the hilltop town of Montalcino is the splendid Abbey Church of Sant'Antimo that sits in stately isolation within the beautiful surrounding countryside. The Abbey is unfinished, and its lengthy history slightly blurred. According to legend, it was built during the eighth century on a spot chosen by the indomitable Charlemagne (*c.* 742/47–814), King of the Franks, who conquered Italy, although some historians claim its foundations are even older than this. However the oldest part of the Abbey to survive is a ninth century door on the facade, while the rest of the Romanesque building dates to the twelfth and thirteenth centuries.

HORTI LEONINI
San Quirico d'Orcia

San Quirico d'Orcia is an ancient town that sits on the northern edge of Val d'Orcia with views across the Orcia and Asso valleys. It is an extraordinary place, often overlooked, and full of delightful 'hidden' treasures including the Horti Leonini, designed in 1580 by Diomede Leoni. These formal gardens lead from the central Piazza della Libertà, and are an exquisite example of sixteenth century Italianate garden design. The focal point of the gardens, which are composed of trim box hedges and rich green ilex, is the pristine statue of Cosimo III de' Medici (1642–1723) that came from the Palazzo Chigi.

COLLEGIATA
San Quirico d'Orcia

From the medieval gateway in San Quirico d'Orcia's walls leads the Via Poliziana, which wends its way past the Palazzo Chigi and towards the Collegiata. This wonderful Romanesque-Gothic church dating to the twelfth and thirteenth centuries was built on the site of a much earlier religious structure. Perhaps most striking of all are the church's three extraordinary portals, of which the south one, pictured, is the finest. This 'portale di mezzogiorno' was designed by either Giovanni Pisano (*c*. 1250–*c*. 1315), or one of his followers, and combines both Romanesque and Gothic features. Notable are the carved Lombardic lions that guard the porch and the two caryatid figures, which have been beautifully crafted.

WELLHEAD OUTSIDE THE COLLEGIATA
San Quirico d'Orcia

Next to the Collegiata stands the impressive and imposing Palazzo Chigi, which was built in 1629 for Cardinal Flavio Chigi, and in the Palazzo's courtyard is a delightful wellhead. Part of San Quirico d'Orcia's charm is its totally unspoilt aspect and tranquillity; at every turn in the small town is a vista of compelling beauty, be that either a simple architectural or sculptural detail such as the well-head, or the stippling of light and shade falling across time-worn building facades, brightened with colourful shutters. The well has some significance since a watercourse used to run below the town.

RURAL CHURCH
near San Quirico d'Orcia

The sight of a small church, flanked by the ever-present cypress trees and perched on the top of a small hillock, is one that is essentially central Tuscan. Here in the heart of Tuscany and far from the bustle of such artistic and cultural meccas as Florence, Siena and Arezzo is the quintessential core of Italy. Across these plains travelled the Etruscans, and those before them, and the Romans, taming and settling this piece of fertile and strategic land. Although much of their culture has disappeared, there is still a sense of the enormity of history here, the tombs uncovered and the artefacts found, that keep the memory of their achievements, cultural, political and artistic, alive.

CYPRESS TREES
near San Quirico d'Orcia

The scenery of the Val d'Orcia and around the town of San Quirico has changed little since the fourteenth century, and is quite distinctive in its appearance with smooth hillocks and vertical stands of cypress trees. This is the landscape that can be easily identified in the backgrounds of many Renaissance paintings, appealing to artists with its aesthetic beauty; sweeping smooth and rolling horizontal lines, broken only by the dark, glossy green of the pointed cypress trees, and mellow stones of ancient medieval settlements. It is an area of Tuscany that has remained totally unspoilt, quiet and away from the beaten track.

TOWARDS THE TOWN
Pienza

Pienza is one of the best examples of a Renaissance-planned town that survives to this day, and was during its time a prototype of the 'ideal' town. The town's evolution is due chiefly to one man, Enea Silvius Piccolomini (1405–64), who was born here and went on to become Pope Pius II. Originally Pienza was called Corsignano and was centred around the Castello di Corsignano, a castle dating to the ninth century and possibly before. After Piccolomini was consecrated Pope in 1458, he set about rebuilding Corsignano as a model Renaissance town and re-named it. This enormous architectural achievement was primarily the work of one architect, Bernardo Gamberelli, known as Rossellino (1409–64).

ROSSELLINO WELL IN PIAZZA PIO II
Pienza

The beautiful well in the Piazza Pio II is essentially the heart of this uniformly Renaissance-planned town. The architect Rossellino based his plan for Pienza around this central Piazza, named after his patron Pope Pius II, who interestingly chose his name from Virgil's *Pius Aeneas*, rather than a religious source. At the centre of the great and elegant piazza stands Rossellino's well, possibly one of the finest of its kind. The well formed the lifeblood of the town, giving the people access to much-needed water, and as such it is rather fitting that it has been treated with such artistry.

ART INSIDE THE DUOMO
Pienza

The splendid duomo was one of the first Renaissance cathedrals to be built, and is an exquisite example of its kind. It is particularly noted for its vast stained-glass windows that allow light to pour into the beautifully proportioned classical interior, and which were specifically requested by Pope Pius II. Housed within the cathedral are a number of art treasures from the Sienese school of painting, including altarpieces by Sano di Pietro (1406–81), Matteo di Giovanni (*c.* 1430–95), Vecchietta (*c.* 1410–80) and Giovanni di Paolo (*c.* 1403–83). Rossellino designed much of the interior, creating a sense of harmony from exterior to interior, with the font and beautifully carved canon stalls being of particular note.

AL FRESCO RISTORANTE
Pienza

The town of Pienza is beautiful, simply without exception. Every detail of the cohesive town was carefully thought out, planned and executed with artistic precision. Weaving through her sun-filled streets and squares today, or sitting at vine-covered terrace ristorantes, is akin to wandering amongst a living work of art. Aside from her architectural fame, Pienza is also noted for her sheep's cheese, Il Pecorino, and annually on the first Sunday of September holds a lively cheese festival. The name of the cheese derives from the word *pecora*, meaning sheep, and it generally has a distinctive sharp and salty taste.

CHURCH OF
MADONNA DI SAN BIAGIO
Montepulciano

Set a short distance from the walls of the hilltop town of Montepulciano is the outstanding Renaissance church of Madonna di San Biagio. As the sun strikes the pale stone exterior the whole building shines with an ethereal luminosity, made more striking by its backdrop of dense, dark green trees. The church was built by the architect Antonio da Sangallo (*c.* 1453–1534), who was responsible for several of the notable buildings in the town itself, and was one of the last great projects he worked on. Begun in 1518, the building plan follows that of the traditional Greek cross, surmounted by an impressive dome, and has an equally harmonious and beautiful interior.

THERMAL WATERS
Bagno Vignoni

The tiny medieval village of Bagno Vignoni, set on a hill
overlooking the Val d'Orcia, has at its centre a beautiful and
large pool, renowned through the centuries for the curative
and restorative powers of its waters. Before the town was
settled and built to its present appearance, the Romans made
use of the spa, whose waters maintain a steady temperature of
52°C (126°F), and since that time they have been visited by a
stream of dignitaries including Pope Pius II (1405–64),
Lorenzo the Magnificent (1449–92) and Grand Duke
Cosimo III (1642–1723).

PIAZZA VECCHIETTA
Castiglione d'Orcia

The tiny, rural and tucked-away village of Castiglione d'Orcia is
another of the region's 'hidden' gems, and sits on a small hilltop
with stunning views across the Val d'Orcia. The streets are steep,
sometimes ending in steps, and wind their way up the incline,
lined on either side by unpainted, tall stone buildings
punctuated by brightly coloured shutters. The main square is
the Piazza Vecchietta, which is also sloping, and was named after
the artist Lorenzo di Pietro (1412–80) who called himself 'Il
Vecchieta'. In the middle of the piazza is a rather fine
Renaissance fountain that dates to 1618.

VIEW FROM THE ROCCA
Castiglione d'Orcia

The village of Castiglione d'Orcia is dominated by the remains
of its impressive 'rocca', or castle, built as a defensive fortress,
which rises up from the midst of the surrounding buildings.
True to its defensive role, the rocca offers spectacular views
across the harmonious jumble of terracotta rooftops in the
village to the Orcia valley. In the distance looms Monte Amiata,
which marks a natural border between central Tuscany and
the long sweep of southern Tuscany that stretches down to the
west coast and to the border of Lazio.

VIA DE LAURA
Cetona

The pretty town of Cetona clings to the edge of its steep hillside
and is presided over by its fortress at the top. Streets wend their
way from the bottom of the town upwards, opening out into
unexpected piazzas, before travelling on up at quite a gradient.
The town plan is circular, as it works its way up the hill, giving
the impression from a distance that the houses are stacked one
on top of the other. Stretching away from the town are fantastic
expanses of open country, lush and brilliant green, heaving with
olive groves, vineyards and the ever-present, dark cypress trees.

CHURCH OF SAN PIETRO
Radicofani

As with so many small towns in central Tuscany, Radicofani
is situated on a small hill, this one rising above the left bank
of the Paglia river. Just beyond the town is the once
omnipotent, though now crumbling, fortress whose history
dates back to the tenth century. The town itself from its lofty
position affords panoramic views across the great basin of
central Tuscany. The main square in Radicofani is dominated
by the thirteenth century Romanesque-Gothic church of
San Pietro, which is particularly notable for its fine works of
art, including an exquisite altarpiece by Andrea della Robbia
(1435–1525), and other works by the della Robbia family.

MEDICI COAT OF ARMS AT VIA CASSIA
Radicofani

Radicofani's long history is littered with battles over its jurisdiction, with Siena and the powerful Medicis of Florence on opposite sides of the field. In 1405 the town came under Sienese rule and a number of buildings and improvements were made, then it fell to the Medici who also stamped their indomitable mark. The presence of the Medici is still strongly felt, especially through the small details such as their coats of arms that appear carved into buildings and monuments. The late Renaissance fountain that stands in front of the Palazzo La Posta on Via Cassia has a particularly fine example carved into its side.

TOWARDS THE TOWN
Abbadia San Salvatore

The little town of Abbadia San Salvatore nestles into the expansive chestnut woods that stretch across the eastern side of Monte Amiata, tucked into the very bottom corner of central Tuscany. The town's wealth was based around her Benedictine Abbey, which was one of the wealthiest and most powerful in Tuscany. According to legend, the Lombard King Rachis founded the abbey in AD 743 on the site where he witnessed a vision, although the building was much added to during the succeeding centuries. In the Middle Ages the Abbey was an important stopping point for pilgrims travelling from Northern Europe to Rome.

SOUTHERN TUSCANY

Stretching from the western slopes of Monte Amiata, westwards to the rugged, picturesque coastline and south, is a piece of Tuscany that still seems to ring with the cries of its most ancient past.

This large area of rolling hills and flat, brilliant blue lakes is largely taken up by the province of Gosseto that corresponds to the region of Maremma, which then spreads on southwards and into Lazio. Perched on the coastline above the sparkling waters of the Mediterranean and once an important Etruscan city and port, is Populonia, home to a venerated Etruscan necropolis, while further along the shore is Ansedonia, a town Roman to its core and rich in artefacts and statuary. Clearly visible from the shore is the large island of Elba with her rich mineral deposits and long history, while further south, in the Tyrrhenian Sea, is the small wine-producing island of Giglio.

Inland is the tiny village of Saturnia, a hidden and glorious jewel within the region. Settled by the Etruscans and turned into a spa town by the Romans, Saturnia's bubbling, thermal waters continue to inspire. The region, whose small villages and towns were largely built on ancient settlements, is home also to magnificent examples of Romanesque, Gothic and Renaissance architecture. There is the elegant town of Pitigliano with its glorious Palazzo Orsini, and small, lovely Montemerano, largely Renaissance in feel; the soft-coloured Magliano in Toscana with her faded Gothic Palazzo dei Priori.

ROCCA
Populonia

ETRUSCAN TOMBS
Populonia

The truly ancient settlement of Populonia is one of Italy's oldest ports, and sits overlooking a bay of brilliant blue waters that stretch into the Mediterranean Sea. Most distinctive from a distance is the silhouette of Populonia's fortress, the Torre di Populonia, which punches its solid shape into the sky, with two crenellated towers, one round and one square. The fortress was built in the fourteenth century, with additions in the fifteenth century by Iacopo Appiani II, with its primary function being to defend the town from pirates. The view from the fortress is quite spectacular, and on fine days Livorno, many miles to the north along the coastline, is visible.

In ancient times Populonia was one of the Etruscans' most important cities and was called Popluna. It was their only city situated on the coast, and it was the centre of their smelted iron ore industry; they extracted the ore from the nearby Island of Elba. The area surrounding Populonia positively breathes with the ancient Etruscan past; there is their necropolis, solemn and stately tombs and many hundreds of artefacts, all of which attest to the thriving economy the town once had, which then suffered a decline under Roman control in around 1000 AD. The town was partially revived during the Middle Ages, but never regained its former Etruscan prestige.

VIEW FROM THE MAINLAND
Island of Elba

The Island of Elba rises from the azure waters of the Mediterranean, clearly visible from the Tuscan coastline and not far from the Etruscan town of Populonia. Elba is rich in iron ore and has through the centuries been an important mining centre, its iron being extracted first by the Etruscans, them the Greeks, Romans and Pisans. In the Middle Ages the island was dominated by the Medici; Cosimo I de' Medici founded the main port and town, building huge defensive structures to prevent pirates plundering the island's resources, and calling the town Cosmopoli. Its name was later changed to Portoferraio.

MARCIANA ALTA
Island of Elba

Elba is the largest island of the Tuscan Archipelago and is part of the National Park of the Tuscan Archipelago. It is around 138 sq km (86 sq miles) in size and is divided into eight communes of which Marciana is one. Secreted away in the hills of Marciana is the beautiful and rustic settlement of Marciana Alta where the spa Fonte di Napoleone can be found. Napoleon Bonaparte (1769–1821) was exiled to Elba in 1814, and spent nine months on the island, during which time he oversaw a number of social reforms and extensive building and planning projects that improved the towns.

COASTLINE AT DAWN
Island of Elba

The Island of Elba, and her surrounding seas are spectacularly
beautiful, perhaps never more so than when seen at dawn
when silver light bathes the landscape. It lends the scene a
particularly magical atmosphere, and it takes just a short leap
of imagination to land in the legends of *Jason the Argonaut*
who is alleged to have landed on Elba at the mythically
named Porto Argo that relates to the island's capital and port
Portoferraio. The port was widely considered one of the
safest in the Mediterranean due to its sheltered location, and
was later greatly reinforced by the Medici.

STREET SCENE
Island of Elba

Despite her healthy tourist industry Elba, has remained unspoilt
and particularly beautiful. The island is divided into eight
communes, whose towns and villages remain quintessentially
ancient in character, with streets that wind down to the
stunning coastline lined by time-faded stone buildings. The
highest mountain on the island is Monte Capanne, from whose
peak there are breathtaking views across the island to the seas
that glitter in the distance. Chestnut woods grow in abundance,
skirting lush, cultivated fields and hovering beyond the reaches
of Elba's smooth, sandy beaches and coves.

TOWARDS THE TOWN
Arcidosso

On the western slopes of Monte Amiata and overlooked by
Monte Labbro is the ancient hillside town of Arcidosso. From a
distance the houses appear clustered together, one on top of the
other as they wend their way along the slope, poking up from
in between densely wooded areas of chestnut trees and beech. It
is an idyllic spot, and the town, with its slightly crumbling but
imposing buildings, dark passageways giving onto small, quaint
piazzas filled with light and archways, retains a sense of faded
and quiet elegance. Arcidosso is first mentioned in the ninth
century, although was probably settled earlier than this, but it
was extensively remodelled during the Renaissance.

ROCCA ALDOBRANDESCA
Arcidosso

The town of Arcidosso is presided over by the ruins of the
Rocca Aldobrandesca, a huge and dominant structure that was
built by the Aldobrandeschi family in around 1000 AD. The
town grew up around the fortress, sheltering within the hulk of
its great walls. The Aldobrandeschi family held power over the
area, using their fortress to ward off attacks from Siena but
finally, after a four-month siege in 1331, the Sienese army
triumphed and the town was taken over. In 1556, after the
Sienese republic collapsed, Aldobrandesca passed to the Medici,
and much evidence of the Florentine rulers remains, with their
coat of arms carved into many of the buildings and monuments.

THERMAL WATERS
Saturnia

Close to the tiny village of Saturnia in the verdant valley of the
Albegna rushes the 'terme di Saturnia', a sulphurous stream of
warm water that tumbles over a series of small falls and on past
an old mill. These waters, that keep an even temperature, were
noted for their allegedly curative powers by the Etruscans and
Romans, and continue to form part of the much-visited
Saturnia spas. The ancient village was settled by the Etruscans
first, evidence of their presence remains through their tombs,
and then by the Romans, who laid out the plan of the town.

CHURCH OF
SANTA MARIA MADDALENA
Saturnia

The Romans named the small village Saturnia after the
God Saturn who, according to legend, threw a thunderbolt
at earth that created a spring of magic warm water. The
Roman foundations of the town are still keenly felt through
the great Etruscan-Roman walls and the typically Roman
configuration of streets. Leading from the large Piazza Vittorio
Veneto is the Romanesque Parish Church, the church of
Santa Maria Maddalena, which is home to a particularly fine
Madonna and Child by Benvenuto di Giovanni (1436–c. 1518)
and exquisite, though damaged, frescos that depict the church
patron kneeling at the feet of St Peter.

PORTA ROMANA
Saturnia

The ancient Roman gate, the Porta Romana, is the main entrance to the charming little village of Saturnia, and has a rather magical feel; shadows stippling the grassy stones and light-drenched fragments of what lies beyond beckon the traveller, enticing one in. It is a secretive and strangely beautiful portal to the village whose streets echo with their ancient history. The gate is tucked within the still partially surviving Etruscan-Roman walls that follow a polygonal form, and Roman and Etruscan artefacts have been excavated from in and around the town.

ROCCA ALDOBRANDESCA
Sovana

The tiny village of Sovana now consists of basically one main street that joins the ruins of the Rocca Aldobrandesca to the duomo, although when it was settled by the Etruscans it was one of their major centres. The town is in a stunning spot, situated high on a ridge that rises from the surrounding plains, and affords breathtaking views over the countryside. In the thirteenth century Sovana came under the power of one branch of the wealthy Aldobrandesca family who built the impressive Rocca during the thirteenth and fourteenth century. Later the village fell to the Sienese, and then to the Medici, but the area succumbed to malaria, forcing the inhabitants to flee to nearby Pitigliano, and the village went into a decline.

ENTRANCE OF THE DUOMO
Sovana

Rather unusually the duomo, which is consecrated to St Peter and
St Paul, stands at the very end of the village in splendid isolation
and shaded by trees. The cathedral was begun in the ninth century,
but was repeatedly added to until the fourteenth century, and
remains a striking mix of Romanesque and Gothic architecture.
Of particular note is the cathedral's doorway, which has unusual
and beautiful carved tracery stonework above the doorway and a
surprising human figure carved in relief on one of the archway
stones. Sovana was also the birthplace of Pope Gregory VII, who
was born in a house along the Via del Duomo in *c.* 1020–25.

SURROUNDING COUNTRYSIDE
Sovana

The views from Sovana across the surrounding countryside are
particularly beautiful; this is part of the province of Grosseto and
also partly the area of Maremma. Here is Tuscany's agricultural
base with extensive ranch-type lands, cattle and crops. The land
is fertile and rich, and wildlife and flora abundant. It is also an
area particularly associated with the Etruscans, and many of
their tombs and ancient settlements still survive in part, dotted
across the rolling landscape. To the west the land slopes towards
the Tyrrhenian Sea and the long, sandy and unspoilt beaches of
Southern Tuscany's coastline.

TOWARDS THE TOWN
Pitigliano

The extraordinary town of Pitigliano perches on the top of a volcanic outcrop that rises from the Lente and Melata river valleys. The town's buildings appear to seamlessly meld with the tufa cliffs on which it sits, and at their lower reaches there are stables and storerooms carved into the cliffs themselves. The defensive qualities of the natural site were recognized and utilized by the Etruscans and the Romans first, and later by the Aldobrandeschi family in the Middle Ages. In 1293 the Orsini family took power and began building the magnificent Palazzo Orsini.

STREET SCENE
Pitigliano

Pitigliano is full of fascinating architectural jewels that attest to the wealth of the town during its heyday, including the aqueduct, built in 1545 by Gian Francesco Orsini to provide the town with water. The structure, which survives with two great arches and thirteen smaller ones, passes with elegance before the imposing Palazzo Orsini. An earlier addition was the Cathedral of St Peter and St Paul, built in the thirteenth century, with an impressive campanile that doubled as a defensive watchtower. On a less lofty, but equally interesting note are the many external staircases in the town, built from beautiful mellowed stone and adding a dynamic twist to the quiet, shade-filled streets.

TOWARDS THE TOWN
Montemerano

Set on the top of a small hill, the town of Montemerano can be seen for many miles, and is an architectural and artistic treasure. Surrounding the town are expansive olive groves with their rows of heavy-leafed, gnarled trees and rolling countryside dotted with sheep. This is an area that still upholds traditional rural crafts, such as the production of wool, and it is not uncommon to see great swatches of wool being prepared outside the stone-built houses in the town. The pace of life here is slow, the streets quiet and unspoilt and the buildings often vine-covered and beautiful.

CHURCH OF SAN GIORGIO
Montemerano

Much of the town of Montemerano is Renaissance in feel, although it was settled long before this. The town's defensive walls were greatly added to during the fifteenth century, and in the same period of time the Chiesa San Giorgio was built. The plain, simple and austere facade of this small church belies the wealth of art treasures concealed within. Amongst these is a particularly fine carved wooden statue of St Peter that has an incredibly animated face and extraordinary detailing in his beard and curling hair. The piece was carved by Lorenzo di Pietro, better known as Il Vecchietta (*c.* 1412–80) who was born in the Tuscan town of Castiglione d'Orcia to the southeast of Siena.

TUSCAN VILLA
Montemerano

The buildings of Montemerano are distinctive through their rustic elegance and their harmonious proportions. Many of the villas have vines creeping across their often crumbling plasterwork or colourful flowers and shrubbery around their doors and windows. The town as a whole is quite beautiful and full of soft-coloured stones, terracotta roof tiles and sun-filled streets. Within her churches are noted art works by artists such as Sano di Pietro (1406–81), Pellegrino di Mariano, Andrea di Niccolò (d. 1483) and Stefano di Giovanni di Sassetta (1392–*c*. 1450/51), while presiding over the town is her leaning medieval tower.

CHURCH OF SAN BRUZIO
Magliano in Toscana

The magical Chiesa San Bruzio seems almost more compelling due to its ruinous state, with grass and shrubs pushing up through its ancient stones, and an air of infinite melancholy. The eleventh-century church sits in isolation beyond the town of Magliano in Toscana, and hidden within long reaches of olive groves. Near to the church is an Etruscan necropolis, being yet another reminder of the incredible impression that the ancient Etruscans made on this part of the country, including first settling the town of Magliano in Toscana.

PALAZZO DEI PRIORI
Magliano in Toscana

Although the hilltop town of Magliano in Toscana dates back to the Etruscans, most of the town's surviving architecture is either Renaissance in style or reminiscent of the Sienese Gothic style. One of the finest buildings to grace the town is the Gothic Palazzo dei Priori, which was built in 1430, and whose slightly crumbling walls attest to its long and inevitably tumultuous history. The stones have faded to an entrancing harmony of soft reds, ochre and grey from which the many coats of arms, carved from smooth grey-white stone stand out. These coats of arms refer to the different Podestas of Magliano, and are a fascinating visual history of the powerful ruling families.

ROMAN REMAINS
Ansedonia

Ansedonia sits on Tuscany's coastline south of the larger town of Orbetello and overlooking the waters of the Busano lagoon and the Tyrrhenian Sea. This ancient town is Roman to its core. Originally called Cosa by the Romans, it was then a large city and was established in around 300 BC. The Roman presence here remains vital and strong, not least in the imposing Roman fortified wall, built with eighteen lookout towers, many of which still stand; this bastion of coastal strength survived many attacks over the centuries, attesting to the strategic placement of the town and the ferocity of its defences.

ART INSIDE THE MUSEO DI COSA
Ansedonia

There are remnants and reminders of the Roman influence on the development of Ansedonia at every turn. The main access to the town is through the Porta Romana, a beautifully preserved gateway that leads to the old Roman forum. Excavations have uncovered a huge wealth of artefacts and even mosaic pavements, wall paintings, villas and statuary, while there is also a Roman canal, dug to join the port with Lake Burano. Nearby is the Torre della Tagliata, where the composer Giacomo Puccini (1858–1924) stayed while writing his famous opera Tosca.

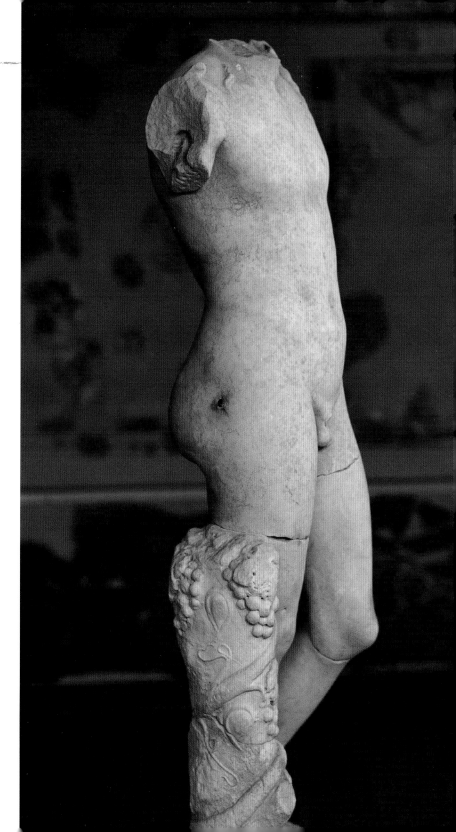

RED LIGHTHOUSE
Island of Giglio

The rocky, mountainous island of Giglio sits surrounded by the brilliant blue waters of the Tyrrhenian Sea not far from the coastline of Tuscany's Grosseto province. The little red lighthouse on one corner of the island provides a vibrant splash of colour against the expansive blue of sea and sky. Giglio is particularly beautiful and rugged, and home to abundant, productive vineyards that produce the local Ansonaco wine. The area, which is also rich in minerals, was settled by the Etruscans and then the Romans, and is home to the remains of a Roman villa.

INDEX